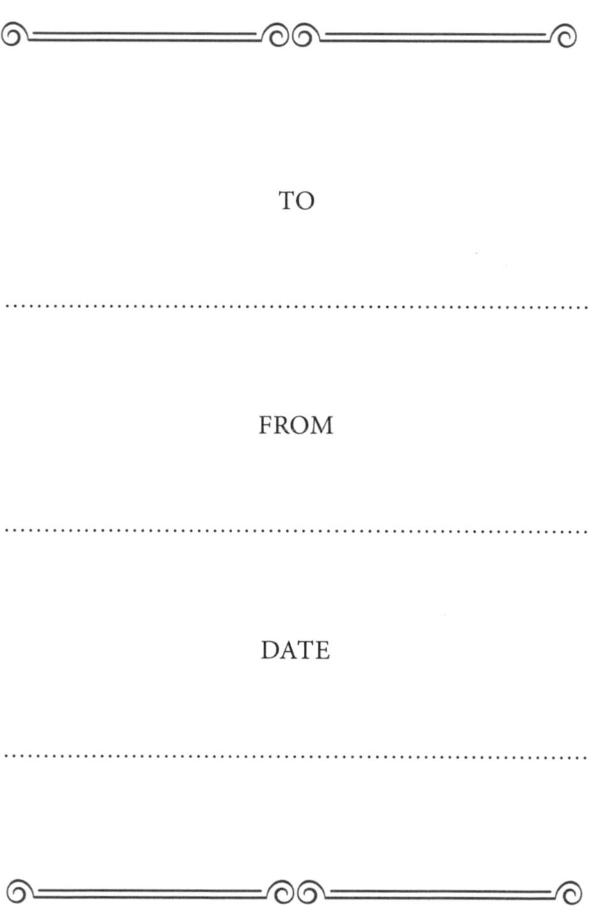

TO

FROM

DATE

GOD'S PROMISES® *Every Day*

Day Devotional

JACK COUNTRYMAN

God's Promises Every Day

Published in Nashville, Tennessee, by Thomas Nelson. Thomas Nelson is a registered trademark of HarperCollins Christian Publishing, Inc.

Thomas Nelson titles may be purchased in bulk for educational, business, fund-raising, or sales promotional use. For information, please e-mail SpecialMarkets@ThomasNelson.com.

ISBN 978-1-4003-2100-1

Printed in China

24 DSC 10 9 8 7 6 5 4 3

INTRODUCTION

Times of change, trouble, or doubt can leave us looking for answers, wondering what God says about our situation. God includes more than seven thousand promises in His Word. As you read through these devotions each day, may God bring you encouragement and assurance through Scripture about the promises He has for your life. It is our hope and prayer that these 365 devotions will bless you as you read and ponder each day.

JANUARY

JANUARY 1

GOD'S PLAN FOR YOU

"For I know the plans I have for you," declares the LORD, *"plans to prosper and not to harm you, plans to give you hope and a future."*

JEREMIAH 29:11 NIV

In Philippians the Lord urges each one of us to live in such a way that we "press toward the goal for the prize of the upward call of God in Christ Jesus" (3:14). And as we begin the new year, we often stop to contemplate and plan just exactly how to do that.

But for all our resolutions, we can achieve a life that reflects *God's* plans for us only if the Lord is front and center in our lives every day. God promises that, when we live for Him, His plans for us are excellent and full of hope. Let this year be a new beginning of living and walking ever closer to our heavenly Father, with great joy in our hearts as we anticipate His plans for us.

Father, I believe You have great and wonderful plans for my life. In this new year, teach me to live closer to You so I might see those plans unfold.

JANUARY 2

GOD GOES WITH YOU

"Be strong and of good courage; do not be afraid, nor be dismayed, for the LORD your God is with you wherever you go."

JOSHUA 1:9

Where will this new year take you? What new journeys, what new adventures, what new challenges will you face? Begin this new year trusting in the Lord, for He will be "with you wherever you go." Call on Him—He is waiting for you to come to Him with open arms.

This year holds many opportunities for fulfillment. Fulfillment in relationships, careers, and interests. But the best and truest fulfillment is found when you focus your thoughts on Jesus Christ. Start each day praising His holy name. Spend time in prayer and in the Word, keeping an open mind and heart. When you do, He will go with you always, and He will bless you beyond your wildest dreams.

Lord, You are my strength and my courage. Because You are ever with me, I can travel in peace.

JANUARY 3

THE LORD GUIDES

The Lord will guide you continually, and . . . you shall be like a watered garden, and like a spring of water, whose waters do not fail.

ISAIAH 58:11

"The Lord will guide you continually"—what a beautiful promise! Each day we can look forward to His Spirit going before, clearing the way, lighting the path, and giving us the guidance we need. His presence is in each circumstance of our lives, whether good or bad. In every moment, He promises to draw us ever closer to Him and to His perfect will for our lives. And He promises to give us all the strength we need to follow Him.

But God doesn't stop at mere survival. He doesn't just satisfy and strengthen. Though there will be difficulties and times of drought in our lives, God guides us to His living waters. He enables us to flourish "like a watered garden," where His blessings always bloom.

Father, when I walk through the deserts of this life, I will trust You to satisfy my thirst. Lead me in the way You wish me to go.

JANUARY 4

GOD LOVES US, PERIOD

God demonstrates His own love toward us, in that while we were still sinners, Christ died for us.

ROMANS 5:8

The guilt that sin brings into our lives is often the stumbling block that keeps us from a deeper walk with God. We fear that when we miss the mark He has set, He is so disappointed that He simply gives up on us. But this verse from Romans tells us that God knew we were sinners—that we would continue to sin—yet He still loved us enough to send His own Son to save us.

The fact is, God stands ready to forgive us when we repent of our sin. His love is unconditional and abundant. Through His forgiveness, He wants us to grow to be more like Jesus. We are not perfect, but our heavenly Father looks beyond our mistakes and calls us to a deeper walk with Him.

Lord, sometimes it's hard to believe that You sent Your perfect Son to die for such an imperfect one as me. Praise You for Your saving love and grace.

JANUARY 5

JESUS GIVES REST

"Come to Me, all you who labor and are heavy laden, and I will give you rest."

MATTHEW 11:28

What a beautiful invitation the Lord offers us! In the midst of whatever trouble or conflict we face—no matter how huge or how trivial—we can go to Jesus. We're not imposing, we're not interrupting. We are wanted and welcome.

So why is it that so often when we face a problem or a challenge, He is the last one we turn to? We flounder along, trying to solve everything on our own, often failing and exhausting ourselves in the process. Jesus is just waiting for us to come to Him. When we develop a deeper relationship with Him, we learn to accept His invitation and surrender our will to His. Then He blesses us with the kind of rest and peace that only He can give. Turn to Him; He truly is the Way (John 14:6).

Lord, You have invited me to come to You with all my burdens, worries, doubts, and cares. I lay myself before You. Bless me with rest for my weary soul.

JANUARY 6

GOD WANTS TO BLESS YOU

Blessed is every one who fears the Lord, *who walks in His ways. . . . You shall be happy, and it shall be well with you.*

PSALM 128:1–2

Do you want to be blessed? Then turn to the Giver of all life's blessings.

Happiness is the desire of everyone's heart. We do everything we can to find it, to earn it, to keep it. But true joy—a joy that soars beyond the boundaries of any earthly happiness—comes to us as a gift when we walk faithfully with our God.

What does that mean? It means we fear the Lord. We give Him the honor and the respect He deserves. We choose to live this day, and every day after, loving and obeying Him. We let His light shine through our lives for all the world to see. And when we do these things, when we walk "in His ways," God blesses with us with life abundant (John 10:10).

Lord, help me be the person You wish me to be. Fill me with Your joy, and bless me that I might bless those around me.

JANUARY 7

GOD IS YOUR REFUGE

The Lord *also will be a refuge for the oppressed,*
a refuge in times of trouble.

PSALM 9:9

"A refuge in times of trouble." That is what God has promised to be for us when we feel besieged, when we need a safe place to wait out the difficulties of life. We who know His name must put our trust in Him, believing in His absolute faithfulness.

God never abandons us, never leaves us on our own to face the dark times. When trouble knocks upon our door; when the mountains we must climb seem too steep; when we find ourselves in deep, drowning waters—He is there. Nothing can keep us from the love of God, and His arms are open to shelter us—every time—when we choose to hope in Him.

Father, when calamity strikes, help me to remember to run straight to You. You are always available to me, my refuge in troubled times.

JANUARY 8

GOD WILL EMPOWER YOU

When you roam, [God's commands] will lead you; when you sleep, they will keep you; and when you awake, they will speak with you.

PROVERBS 6:22

When we experience hardships, it may make us question God's will for our lives. And while we may be unclear about careers or losses or relationships, we must always remember that the most important thing in life is living in a way that pleases and glorifies our heavenly Father and His Son.

God tells us about the kind of life that pleases Him: love Him with all we are (Mark 12:30), love our neighbor (Matthew 22:39), and live out a love that reflects Jesus (1 Corinthians 13).

God will enable us to live according to these commands. He will empower us as we earnestly seek to live out His will, to love Him, and to love others.

Lord, I'm not sure exactly what's happening in my life right now, or what I'm supposed to do about it. But I do know that I will keep loving You and loving others, no matter what.

JANUARY 9

GOD IS OUR TREASURE

"Lay up for yourselves treasures in heaven, where neither moth nor rust destroys and where thieves do not break in and steal. For where your treasure is, there your heart will be also."

MATTHEW 6:20–21

Treasure. What does that word mean to you? For some, it calls up images of a pirate's chest brimming with gold and precious stones. For others, it's big bank accounts, a bigger house, and the biggest, fanciest, grown-up toys. But the real question is, how does God define treasure? That forces us to decide what is an earthly treasure and what is a heavenly one.

Jesus tells us that those things moths and rust can destroy are earthly treasures, and they do not last. Our heavenly treasures are the promised riches of our Father's love, His saving mercy, and His unmerited, boundless grace. Those are the treasures that last for all eternity. And *those* are the treasures we are to seek.

Lord, I do thank You for the earthly treasures You've given me, but I pray You would teach my heart to cherish Your heavenly treasures above all else.

JANUARY 10

GOD NEVER LEAVES US

The Lord, He is the One who goes before you. He will be with you, He will not leave you nor forsake you.

DEUTERONOMY 31:8

Have you ever been left alone? Left to find your own way, fight your own battles? Have you ever been forsaken by family, by friends, by those you thought would stand by you? Then you know the power of this promise: "[God] will not leave you nor forsake you."

When life darkens our door with its troubles and trials, Satan wants nothing more than for us to feel forsaken and alone—but we are not! God stands by our side; He guides, counsels, and comforts. Rest assured, no matter what you face in the coming year, *nothing* can separate you from the love of your Father (Romans 8:38–39). Therefore walk boldly into each new day, knowing that you follow the footsteps of the One who never leaves you.

Lord, when I feel lost and alone, remind me that You are there. Help me to sense Your presence and leading in my life.

JANUARY 11

CHRIST RECONCILES US

If when we were enemies we were reconciled to God through the death of His Son, much more, having been reconciled, we shall be saved by His life.

ROMANS 5:10

When we were enemies . . . to God." Do those words give your heart pause? How does it feel to know that you—before you trusted in Christ as your Savior—were an enemy of God? And how does it feel to know that, despite the enmity between you, He sent His Son to die for your sins anyway? Romans 5:8 says it this way: "God demonstrates His own love toward us, in that while we were still sinners, Christ died for us."

If God demonstrated that depth of love through the death of His Son, what will He do through the life of His risen Son? In this glorious promise, Paul tells us, "We shall be saved by His life." Not merely saved *from* sin, but saved *to* a heavenly and eternal home with Him.

Father, thank You for not only saving me from sin, but saving me to Your side.

JANUARY 12

THE PRIZE IS HEAVEN

I press toward the goal for the prize of the upward call of God in Christ Jesus.

PHILIPPIANS 3:14

We are daily in the race of life. We stumble, learn from our mistakes, start again, and try to run better from there on. Meanwhile God has called us to leave our mistakes behind us, to forget the stumblings of the past, and to make serving Christ our goal.

Through His Word, the Lord urges us to run the race of life in such a way that we may obtain the prize of the "imperishable crown" (1 Corinthians 9:25) of heaven. To do this, we must run with endurance while looking to Jesus (Hebrews 12:1–2), who doesn't leave us to run alone. Rather He is our constant Companion, running alongside and giving us the strength and encouragement we need to keep running the race.

Father, empower me to run the race in a prize-winning way. Fill me with Your Spirit that my life will reflect Your love, endurance, and tenacity.

JANUARY 13

GUARD YOUR TONGUE

Set a guard, O Lord, over my mouth; keep watch over the door of my lips.

PSALM 141:3

Like a double-edged sword, the tongue can build up or tear down, beautify or destroy, heal or hurt. So mighty a weapon should be unsheathed only by the Master's hand. Yet how often are we tempted to wield that weapon with only our own wisdom—or lack thereof—to guide us? Through David's example in Psalm 141, God encourages us to call upon Him to "keep watch over the door of [our] lips."

With our tongue, we can either curse men or praise the Lord. Choose to fill your thoughts with things that are good and pure and holy (Philippians 4:8). Then consciously let your words reflect those thoughts, bringing glory to His holy name.

Lord, guard my tongue so everything I say is a reflection of Your love.

JANUARY 14

GOD SUPPLIES OUR NEEDS

My God shall supply all your need according to His riches in glory by Christ Jesus.

PHILIPPIANS 4:19

Financial difficulties can turn our focus inward and build up incredible stress and anxiety. We can feel suffocated by outstanding bills and preoccupied with trying to figure out how we will ever pay them. Turning to God for wisdom and direction is vital to every step we take toward financial freedom.

God's Word is filled with the knowledge and insight we need for getting through these tough times. He knows the demands we face. And He has promised to supply all our needs according to the riches of His perfect knowledge, unlimited power, and unshakable love for us. As He gives to us, we must also remember to give back to Him—with our time, our talents, and yes, even our money. When we trust God enough to give, He rewards us in ways we can't even imagine.

Lord, I do believe You will provide me with everything I truly need. Thank You!

JANUARY 15

A PLACE FOR YOU

"In My Father's house are many mansions. . . . I go to prepare a place for you."

JOHN 14:2

Think about this truth: there is a place in heaven prepared for you. And what a wonderful promise! In heaven, we will at last find our true home. We will have peace and rest. Never again will we be troubled by pain or sorrow. Every sin, every heartache, every moment of struggle will all fade away. And we will live forever with God in glory.

Therefore let us not be bogged down by the worries and weariness this life can sometimes hold. Instead, let's fill our minds with thoughts of that place prepared just for us. Let's allow His presence to seep into every corner of our hearts. Let's choose to live each moment of this day *for* God—until that wonderful day when we can live each moment *with* God.

Lord, how comforting it is to know You have prepared a special place for me in heaven. I praise You, Lord, for the promise of my new home.

JANUARY 16

ON GOD'S MIND

Your thoughts toward us . . . are more than can be numbered.

PSALM 40:5

It's wonderful to know someone is thinking of you, isn't it? Perhaps on your birthday or another special occasion, or perhaps for no particular reason at all. It's just nice to know you're remembered.

Consider this: there has never been a moment when you were not on God's mind. God has never stopped thinking of you. He cares about you so much that He wants to ensure that you have a future and a hope. He plans, provides, protects. He sent His Son to save you and His Spirit to live inside you so that not only are you ever in His thoughts, you are ever in His presence.

Because God always includes you in His thoughts, this day, strive to always include Him in yours.

Lord, when I try to imagine that You—the God of all creation—consider me, I am overwhelmed with thanksgiving.

JANUARY 17

GOD GIVES PEACE

Don't worry about anything. . . . Tell God what you need, and thank him for all he has done. Then you will experience God's peace.

PHILIPPIANS 4:6–7 NLT

Our Father loves us. And because He loves us, He does not want our hearts to be anxious or our lives to be filled with worry. So He offers us the gift of prayer, asking that we not only accept His gift but use it. The more we include God in our lives, the more He becomes a part of everything we say and do.

The Lord has a place and a purpose in His kingdom for each of us—and it's not a place of worry or fear. When we open our hearts to God's leading, letting Him guide our every choice along the way, He not only shapes us into who He created us to be, but He also fills us with a bold confidence and a peace so great we simply cannot comprehend them.

Father, I lay my life before You. Fill me with Your purpose and Your promised peace that passes all understanding.

JANUARY 18

BEGIN WITH GOD

The Sovereign Lord is on my side!

ISAIAH 50:9 NLT

In every life there come times when we face an obstacle we just cannot overcome on our own. We all need *help*. And while family and friends are wonderful and priceless, they can't be all places at all times. Their strength is not limitless, and they cannot make the impossible possible. But God can.

When troubles come our way—whether big or small, extraordinary or everyday—the solution begins with God: "Look to the Lord and his strength" (1 Chronicles 16:11 NIV). He hears every prayer and begins answering before we even finish speaking. In His perfect wisdom, He gives guidance, courage, and strength. He offers shelter, comfort, and peace. Look to the Lord—He is on your side.

Holy Father, I know You are the answer to all my problems. Thank You for Your help.

JANUARY 19

GOD'S LOVE IS FOR US

Though I walk in the midst of trouble, . . .
Your right hand will save me.

PSALM 138:7

David trusted God—a fact painted by the words of this psalm. Whether in the "midst of trouble" or facing the "wrath of [his] enemies" (v. 7), David knew the Lord would keep him safe and would make right all that was wrong (v. 8).

And in the perfect hindsight of a few thousand years, we might think that David couldn't possibly understand what we face today. But couldn't he? Office politics, relational insecurities, family strife: David faced all those things and more. But David the king was confident in the Lord his King. And we can be too because that same covenant of love between David and God is ours to claim. The Lord's steadfast "love endures forever" (Psalm 136:1 NIV)—and that love is for us, children of the King.

Lord, no matter what happens in my life, You will protect me and save me. I will be forever faithful to You.

JANUARY 20

GOD SANCTIFIES US

May the God of peace Himself sanctify you completely; and may your whole spirit, soul, and body be preserved blameless at the coming of our Lord Jesus Christ.

1 THESSALONIANS 5:23

The more time we spend studying God's Word, the more often we come to Him in prayer, the more times we sacrifice our desires to His will—the closer to Him we will become. Why is that important? Because even though our God is the King of the universe, His greatest desire is to have each of us stand sanctified and blameless by His side for all eternity (2 Peter 3:9). That happens when we commit all of who we are to the Lord. In return, He sets us apart from this fallen world and makes us holy—no, not perfect, but wholly His.

This day, allow God to be the center of everything you think and do. Embrace His promise; be sanctified and wholly His.

Lord, because of Your sacrifice on the cross, I can stand blameless before You. Words cannot express my thankfulness.

JANUARY 21

GOD GIVES WISDOM

If any of you lacks wisdom, let him ask of God, who gives to all liberally and without reproach, and it will be given to him.

JAMES 1:5

The wisdom of the world says, "Me first," "If it feels good, do it," and "More is better."

But the wisdom of God is altogether different—it is "first pure, then peaceable, gentle, willing to yield, full of mercy and good fruits, without partiality and without hypocrisy" (James 3:17). And what a difference godly wisdom can make—not only in our lives, but in the world around us.

The question then is how to get godly wisdom in a world that advises us to "do unto others *before* they can do unto us." The answer is simple: ask God. Ask, and He promises to give—"liberally and without reproach." God isn't stingy. And He doesn't berate us for not knowing what to do. Instead, when we go to Him, He lovingly fills us with all the wisdom we will ever need.

Lord, grant me Your wisdom so I might live a life pleasing in Your sight.

JANUARY 22

GOD FORGIVES

"If you forgive those who sin against you, your heavenly Father will forgive you."

MATTHEW 6:14 NLT

If we want to be forgiven of our sins, we must go to God and confess them. Then "He is faithful and just to forgive us our sins and to cleanse us from all unrighteousness" (1 John 1:9). But that's not all we must do. There's one more thing: we must forgive too.

The secret to a peaceful life—with your family, your friends, the world around you—is to be willing to forgive those who offend you and cause you grief and pain. God never wants us to hold on to our anger or nurture a grudge. He knows that true healing, both for ourselves and the one who hurt us, begins with forgiveness. In order to receive His promised gift, we must also give it to others.

Lord, forgiving is not always an easy thing to do. Please work in my heart and create a willingness to forgive those who have wronged me.

JANUARY 23

WE HAVE A HELPER

"If you love Me, keep My commandments. And I will pray the Father, and He will give you another Helper."

JOHN 14:15–16

As Jesus was preparing His disciples for His return to heaven, He gave them this message: "If you love Me, keep My commandments."

The disciples had walked with Jesus, watched Him serve, and listened to His teachings. But He was about to leave them, and Jesus knew they would struggle to obey on their own. So He promised, "I will pray the Father, and He will give you another Helper." And the Holy Spirit of God came to live inside the disciples.

When we become followers of Christ, that same Spirit comes to live inside us, to teach us about God's Word, pray for us, and help us in our weaknesses (John 14:26, 16:13; Romans 8:26–27). He equips us to obey the Lord so our lives reflect His love for us . . . and our love for Him.

Father, thank You for sending the Holy Spirit, the Helper, to teach, to guide, and even to pray for me.

JANUARY 24

GOD DELIVERS US

You have lovingly delivered my soul from the pit of corruption, for You have cast all my sins behind Your back.

ISAIAH 38:17

Troubles are never pleasant at the time, but they quickly turn into tools when entrusted to God. Our Lord will take our times of troubles and trials—even the hard feelings we experience in them—and use them to teach us to fully rely on Him and His provision.

Whether we're confronted with divorce, death, or loss of our worldly possessions, the Lord will carry us through. He will provide all we truly need. But our loving God does more than merely rescue us "from the pit"; He casts all our sins and missteps behind us and delivers the grace of His blessings. He grants us a new beginning, fresh with opportunities to worship, to serve, to live for Him. The Lord is our Shepherd, and every day we are blessed with His love, mercy, and grace—even amid the darkened days of despair.

On the days when all seems dark, remind me, Lord, that You are faithful.

JANUARY 25

JESUS STILL SERVES

"The Son of Man did not come to be served, but to serve."

MATTHEW 20:28

In our money-driven world, leadership is too often about who has the most power, who "lords" over the most people. But for the Christian leader, there is no room for that kind of thinking. Why? Because Jesus took a very different view of how leaders should lead. Not from a sense of superiority but from a desire to serve.

When Jesus stood up from the lowly task of washing His disciples' feet, He said, "I have given you an example, that you should do as I have done to you" (John 13:15). For all of His life on earth, Jesus served the sick, the poor, the sinful. He died to serve; He rose to serve. In a world distracted by money and power, Jesus promises to continue to serve, to wash His children—not our feet, but our sin-stained souls—until we are whiter than snow.

Lord, thank You for Your example. Place within me a servant's heart that I may bless others.

JANUARY 26

MEASURE OF FAITH

God has dealt to each one a measure of faith.

ROMANS 12:3

God has called each of us to His kingdom for a purpose. So we can fulfill that purpose, He has given us a "measure of faith." This simply means God will enable us to do whatever He has called us to do.

For us, that means two things. First, there is the wonderful promise that God will never ask us to do anything without also giving us what we need to do it. We can step out in faith, knowing He will support us. But it also means that whatever we achieve is not of our own doing; it is God's. So we have no business boasting. We are called to lift up others and to glorify God—not ourselves.

So, child of God, step out in faithful service, trusting God to give you all you need to satisfy His purpose for you.

Lord, empower me to perform steadfast service for You.

JANUARY 27

GOD PROTECTS US

Let us cast off the works of darkness, and let us put on the armor of light.

ROMANS 13:12

Satan has one goal: to destroy our faith and draw us away from the Lord. But God knows how to defeat the evil one. In His Word, He tells us to resist the devil and he will flee from us (James 4:7).

How do we resist? By "[casting] off the works of darkness" and refusing to succumb to the sins and temptations of the world. By clothing ourselves instead in "the armor of light"—the armor of right living and obedience to our God (Romans 13:12).

We live in a world darkened by sin, but God promises that a new day is on its way. Jesus is coming again, and each day brings us closer to His return. Until that joyous day, God shields us with His armor of light from the enemy of our souls.

Help me, Lord, to stand strong against the evil one by living the way You want me to.

JANUARY 28

A REASON TO SHOUT FOR JOY

Let all those rejoice who put their trust in You; let them ever shout for joy.

PSALM 5:11

Happiness and joy are not one and the same. Happiness is based on life's circumstances; joy is not. The root of the word *happiness*—*hap*—is a Middle English word that means "chance." We can feel *happy* when life *chances* to be going well. There is nothing inherently wrong with happiness; it simply pales in comparison to joy.

As believers we can know joy even in the midst of suffering. Joy takes in the big-picture perspective, embracing Jesus' death on the cross, the forgiveness of our sin, and the promise of eternal life with the almighty and holy God in heaven, a place without pain or tears, without sadness or suffering. Unlike happiness, joy isn't dependent upon our circumstances; it's dependent upon Jesus—and that's a reason to shout with joy!

Lord, help me seek Your true and everlasting joy.

JANUARY 29

GOD KNOWS YOUR HEART

Search me, O God, and know my heart . . .
lead me in the way everlasting.

PSALM 139:23–24

God does not leave us to figure out life on our own. Instead, when we don't understand what's happening—in the world around us or in our own hearts and minds—or when we simply don't know which way to go, God offers all the help we need to sort out our choices and attitudes. He knows the deepest secrets and intents of our hearts—and in ways we simply cannot comprehend, He has all the answers we seek.

Our God is not cold and distant; He is intensely personal. He knows our every thought, everything that worries and frightens us, that keeps us staring up at the ceiling in the still-dark hours of the morning. And knowing all those things, God does not turn away. When we open our hearts to God, He guides us and leads us "in the way everlasting."

Lord, search me and take away anything that pulls me away from You.

JANUARY 30

ENDLESS INTERCESSION

He always lives to make intercession for them.

HEBREWS 7:25

S*ome things never change.* That's how the old saying goes, and it sounds a bit pessimistic, almost sighing at the seemingly inescapable troubles of daily life. But it's also true that some good things never change, infinitely joyful and hope-filled things. Consider the steadfast faithfulness of our God. The unending love behind His sacrifice. The unceasing intercession of Christ for us.

Think about that last one for a moment. For though we have chosen to become children of God, we are not perfect; there is still sin in our lives. But imagine this scene: Jesus standing before the throne of His Father and saying, *Yes, Father, she did that. And yes, he said that. But I've already paid the price. They are Mine, and they are set free.*

Lord Jesus, thank You for Your unending prayers and intercession for me.

JANUARY 31

JESUS WORKS THROUGH YOU

"I am the vine, you are the branches. . . .
Without Me you can do nothing."

JOHN 15:5

Jesus is the Vine; we are His branches. And like branches, we can participate in and contribute to His kingdom only when we are connected to Him. If we cut ourselves off from Christ, we are powerless to accomplish anything for Him or for His kingdom. But connected to Christ, we not only discover our abilities, we find ourselves emboldened by His promise to equip us to do His will (Hebrews 13:21).

Have you ever asked the Lord to place someone in your life, someone you can help? If you want to bear fruit, if you want to make a difference for the Lord, ask Him to give you an opportunity to witness for His glory and then watch what happens. Don't worry about what to say or do. Our Savior, the Vine, promises to empower His branches to bear much fruit. Jesus *will* work though you.

Lord, please work through my life so more people will come to know You as their Lord and Savior.

FEBRUARY

FEBRUARY 1

GOD PROMISES TO LOVE

"'Love the Lord your God with all your heart, with all your soul, with all your mind, and with all your strength.' . . . 'Love your neighbor as yourself.'"

MARK 12:30–31

Under the old covenant, there were the Ten Commandments—and all those other hundreds of laws and traditions to follow. Under the new covenant, God neatly bundles them into just two commandments. Those two commandments, however, are so powerful, so far-reaching that they encompass all the other laws.

First, we are to love God with all we are—all our hearts, souls, minds, and strength. God is to reign over every area of our lives. Then we are to love our neighbors, not casually, but just as we love ourselves. Notice what we are *not* commanded to love: houses, fame, fortune, careers, the "stuff" of this world.

With the new covenant, God freed us from the burden of all those laws. Love God. Love others. It really is that simple.

Lord, You have commanded me to love. Place within my heart the desire to live out these commandments.

FEBRUARY 2

OUR HEARTS' DESIRE

Delight yourself also in the LORD, and He shall give you the desires of your heart.

PSALM 37:4

Our God is a loving God, but He isn't Santa Claus or a genie in a bottle. Our God loves to give good gifts, but in His economy the best gifts are not tangible or material. Yes, our God feels compassion when we hurt, but He still allows hardships into our lives that will refine our character and strengthen our faith.

Against the backdrop of these truths, we can better understand the often-misread statement that God will give us the desires of our hearts. The real promise of this verse is that, as we pray, read His Word, and grow closer to the Lord, He will change our hearts so that what we desire for ourselves is what He desires for us. Such a loving God is easy to delight in.

Lord, sift my heart. Make my desires a reflection of Your desires so I may always please You.

FEBRUARY 3

THE FLAME OF FAITH

[Be] fervent in spirit, serving the Lord.

ROMANS 12:11

It can slip up on us so easily that we might not even notice it for a while: complacency about our relationship with Jesus. Life's hurts and demands can put our spiritual health on a back burner, until one day we find that we're just going through the motions of following Jesus.

Recognizing these symptoms is a sign of dissatisfaction with our spiritual status quo. For a fresh start right now, we must first confess to God our need for Him. Then we should do those things we did in the beginning, when we were so "on fire" for God (Revelation 2:5). We must dive into His Word, letting His truth renew our hearts and minds. We must recommit to making Him the priority in our lives. Even when we're unaware that our faith is flickering, God can and will reignite the flame.

Lord, please create a fresh desire within me to draw closer to You, to follow You, to tell others about You.

FEBRUARY 4

ALL THINGS

He who did not spare His own Son, but delivered Him up for us all, how shall He not with Him also freely give us all things?

ROMANS 8:32

Think about this truth for a moment: If God was willing to send His only Son to die a cruel death for our sins, is there anything He would not do to help His children succeed in their walk with Him? Is there any need He would not meet? Any enemy He would not defeat?

Once we have accepted God's offer to become a part of His family, His kingdom, nothing can ever separate us from His love—"neither death nor life, nor angels nor principalities nor powers, nor things present nor things to come, nor height nor depth, nor any other created thing" (Romans 8:38–39). And once God has declared us "Not guilty," no one—not even the devil himself—can change that decree.

Lord, I cannot fathom a love so great that You willingly sacrificed Your own Son. Thank You, with all my heart.

FEBRUARY 5

GOD'S WORD ENCOURAGES

Let the word of Christ dwell in you richly.

COLOSSIANS 3:16

The Word of God—whether written or read, sung out in song or shouted out in praise—is living and powerful (Hebrews 4:12). Like a light in the darkness, it guides our way. It teaches us not only what we should do, but who we should be. It points out our sins and mistakes and guides us back to God.

We must never be stingy with God's Word; instead our lives should be rich with it—with its principles, praises, and promises. We should meditate on it day and night (Joshua 1:8), never allowing it to become just an afterthought or a last resort.

When we spend time in God's Word each day, His truths fill us with His purpose and His peace, giving us hope and encouragement as we walk in God's way.

Father, "open my eyes, that I may see wondrous things from Your law" (Psalm 119:18).

FEBRUARY 6

GOD LIFTS THE HUMBLE

Be submissive to one another, and . . . humble yourselves under the mighty hand of God, that He may exalt you in due time.

1 PETER 5:5–6

Humility is the key that admits us into a closer walk with God. When we humble ourselves before the Lord—when we admit that maybe we don't know everything and His way really is best—He pulls us into His arms and wraps us tightly in His love, drawing us closer to His heart.

God has called us not only to humble ourselves before Him, but also to "be submissive to one another," to put others' needs before our own. Why? Because as we choose to put others first—as we offer them kindness, mercy, and grace—we give them a glimpse of the heart of our God. Our actions invite them to seek Him and give them the hope of His forgiving love. So while we may live the humble life of a servant here on earth, one day, at the right time, God will lift us up.

Father, teach me to serve You and all those around me with a gentle and humble heart.

FEBRUARY 7

GOD PROTECTS YOU

The Lord himself watches over you! The Lord stands beside you as your protective shade.

PSALM 121:5 NLT

In Psalm 121, God gives us a beautiful and endlessly reassuring promise: He will protect us from evil. Like the shadow of our own right hand, He never leaves our side, keeping us from harm day and night. Don't just race past that truth. Stop and consider it: the Lord Himself shields His children.

And God's protection isn't reserved for only the heroes of the faith, the greatest teachers, or the most gifted scholars. He watches over each of His children—yes, you too; no one is overlooked or forgotten. He never takes a vacation or a sick day; He never naps on the job (v. 4). Therefore we can live boldly, confident in His constant care. His protection is more than a hope; it's a promise.

Lord, thank You for being my ever-watchful, ever-present Protector. I give myself to You for Your keeping.

FEBRUARY 8

OUR DESIRE TO GROW

A wise man will hear and increase learning.

PROVERBS 1:5

Growing in our knowledge of Jesus Christ is essential to our walk with God. The Lord does not hide Himself from us; rather He wants us to learn more about Him, His Word, and His Son, Jesus, throughout our lives.

Walking closely with Jesus and being filled with knowledge and wisdom happen only when we read and ponder God's Word, when we spend deliberate and daily time with Him in prayer. As we get to know God better through His Word, we become more sensitive to His leading. It becomes easier for Him to steer our course rightly as we practice obeying Him. Growing in our knowledge of God's Word not only blesses us, it also glorifies Him. The desire to grow spiritually is very much in line with God's will, and as we do our part, He will do His.

Lord, I want to know You better today than I did yesterday, and better tomorrow than I do today.

FEBRUARY 9

GOD GIVES ETERNAL LIFE

God has given us eternal life, and this life is in His Son. He who has the Son has life.

1 JOHN 5:11–12

Eternal life is a gift from God—and we can receive it only through His Son. We cannot earn it, only humbly accept it. How? By believing in Jesus, confessing that He is the Son of God and the Lord of our lives, repenting of our sins, and then choosing to follow and obey Him.

When we choose Jesus, not only does eternal life in heaven becomes ours, but in this life we also receive grace and mercy, courage and strength, comfort and peace, love and joy. John 10:10 says, "I have come that they might have life, and that they may have it more abundantly." Jesus came not only to save us for eternity but to bless our lives today.

Because we have the Son, we have life—and all the gifts that come with it.

Lord, this day and every day, I choose You to be Lord of my life. Thank You for Your saving grace.

FEBRUARY 10

GOD SUSTAINS YOU

Cast your burden on the Lord, and He shall sustain you;
He shall never permit the righteous to be moved.

PSALM 55:22

To whom do you turn when you are troubled? Whom do you call when disaster comes knocking on your door? When enemies pop up out of nowhere and attack? When those you thought were friends turn against you?

Do you say as David did, "I will call upon God"? And do you believe God's promise as David did, "The Lord shall save me" (Psalm 55:16)?

We can cast all our burdens—the worries, the troubles, the disasters, the betrayals, the fears—on the Lord. The Lord who once bore all our sins still offers to carry all our sorrows. We can depend on Him. He will not allow His children to be moved outside His grace. When we are burdened, the Lord God Himself will sustain us.

Father, I lay all my worries and troubles at Your feet, knowing You will hold me safely in Your grace.

FEBRUARY 11

TRANSFORM YOUR LIFE

We all, with unveiled face, beholding as in a mirror the glory of the Lord, are being transformed into the same image from glory to glory.

2 CORINTHIANS 3:18

God desires that our lives be completely refreshed and made new. He's not looking just for improved behavior; He wants to see us re-created from the inside out (2 Corinthians 5:17). That transformation begins when we first surrender our lives to Jesus, and it continues as we develop the character of Jesus by imitating Him and learning His teachings.

As we try to follow Jesus' example, we find it's no easy, overnight process. Rather it's a gradual changing, often requiring sacrifice and struggle, as we learn to reflect His character.

God's work in us continues our whole lives. He lovingly and patiently continues the process of transformation until His work is perfected when Jesus returns to claim His own (Hebrews 12:2).

Lord, I pray that my life would be an ever-brighter, ever-clearer reflection of Your love and glory.

FEBRUARY 12

GOD GIVES COMPASSION

The Lord is gracious and full of compassion,
slow to anger and great in mercy.

PSALM 145:8

The idea of submitting has gotten a bad rap. But depending on whom we choose to submit to, that decision can be the best we ever make. Naming Jesus as our Lord is an act of submitting to Him, but consider the nature of the God we have chosen to serve.

God's nature is one of love and compassion. So it is not in His character to force our submission, as a master would a slave. Rather He seeks our submission, the way a loving Father would a beloved child. He longs for us to come to Him, to obey Him willingly. And when we do, He graciously casts away our confessed sins. Instead of angering at our obstinate and self-centered ways, He offers mercy and grace. And because our Lord is so gracious, it is a joy to submit our lives to Him.

Lord, You are full of grace and compassion.
Help me be more like You.

FEBRUARY 13

NO MORE TEARS

God will wipe away every tear from their eyes. . . . There shall be no more pain.

REVELATION 21:4

The Bible doesn't tell us a lot about heaven—perhaps it's just too wonderful to put into words. The things it does tell us are the very things our souls so long for. No sorrow or death, no pain or crying. "God will wipe away every tear," and all the sad, bad, and evil things of this world will be no more.

In heaven, all things will be made new (Revelation 21:5). All the hollow places of our hearts will be filled, all the shadows chased away by His light, every tear wiped away by our Father's hand. But as wonderful as all that will be, a still greater wonder awaits us in heaven: the privilege of standing in the presence of our almighty Father. To bow before Him, to see His face, to hear Him say, "Well done"—that is the true treasure of heaven.

To step into Your presence, Lord, to feel You brush away my tears, what a wonderful day that will be.

FEBRUARY 14

GOD ABIDES IN US

God is love, and he who abides in love abides in God, and God in him.

1 JOHN 4:16

God is love. And so to abide in God is to abide—*to live*—within the circle of His love. Could there be any place more wonderful?

The place isn't struggle-free, but there we're with One who gives us the courage and strength to succeed in our struggles (Philippians 4:13). It's not sorrow-free, but we're side by side with the One who fills us with a joy and peace that surpasses circumstances (Philippians 4:7). And no, it isn't trouble-free, but we're in the presence of One who walks with us through the fires and does not allow us to be consumed (Isaiah 43:2). When we abide within the circle of God and His love, the Lord God, almighty and all-powerful, abides within us.

Lord Jesus, teach me to follow You. Abide in me so that I may always abide in You.

FEBRUARY 15

HEAVEN IS FOR SINNERS

Not by works of righteousness which we have done,
but according to His mercy He saved us.

TITUS 3:5

Mercy. We don't deserve it. We haven't done—can't possibly do—anything to earn it. And yet we are promised that this unbelievably lavish gift is ours when we choose to follow Jesus.

Why? Why would such a perfect and powerful God give such a gift to ones so undeserving? He tells us in Titus 3:4: because of "the kindness and love of God our Savior toward man." And He not only gave us mercy, He also "poured out on us abundantly" His own Holy Spirit (v. 6), to live and work within us, making us more and more like the Savior who died to save us.

Let's fill our lives with good works to honor our merciful God.

Lord, thank You for the mercy and grace that save me.

FEBRUARY 16

A HOME SECURITY SYSTEM

Whoever listens to me will dwell safely, and will be secure, without fear of evil.

PROVERBS 1:33

We take elaborate measures to ensure the security of our homes and possessions. But too often we neglect the simplest and most effective measure of securing our own souls—turning to God.

So many in our world fail to seek God's wisdom. Instead, they strive to satisfy their own selfish passions without a thought for how their actions impact the future or those around them. For Christians this is spiritually irresponsible. If we try to live apart from the counsel of God's wisdom, we will end up suffering disillusionment, fear, doubt, worry, and frustration.

Our lives often fall apart when we do not involve the Lord in our decisions. If we truly want to secure our souls, we must seek God daily for His plan, direction, and spiritual insight for our lives.

Father, today I ask for Your insight into my life. Show me the way to keep my soul safely and securely in You.

FEBRUARY 17

GOD IS FAITHFUL

If we confess our sins, He is faithful and just to forgive us our sins and to cleanse us from all unrighteousness.

1 JOHN 1:9

God is faithful. He does what He says He will do. He keeps every promise He makes.

One of those promises is that if we confess our sins, He will forgive us. But we tend to focus on His part of the promise and conveniently forget our part—confession.

We *must* confess our sins—the big ones, the little ones, the ones we thought no one knew about. And yes, even the ones we told ourselves weren't really sins at all. Each day our prayer should be: "Search me, O God, and know my heart; . . . see if there is any wicked way in me" (Psalm 139:23–24). And as He reveals our sins, we confess them, agreeing with Him that they are indeed wrong, repent, and believe. Then can we savor His beautiful, promised forgiveness.

Lord, thank You for ensuring my forgiveness.
Today I need to confess . . .

FEBRUARY 18

WE *CAN* PLEASE GOD

Walk in love, as Christ also has loved us and given Himself for us, an offering and a sacrifice to God for a sweet-smelling aroma.

EPHESIANS 5:2

Our God is not some fickle, capricious, changeable sort of God. He does not search out ways to be angry or displeased with His people. In fact, He so wants to be pleased with us that He gave us the example of His Son to follow.

Christ loved us and gave Himself for us. His sacrifice was a "sweet-smelling aroma" to God, and we are to be imitators of Him, to "walk continually in love" (Ephesians 5:1–2)—to value those around us, to offer them compassion and kindness—just as Christ did. We are to love unselfishly and forgive unreservedly, just as Christ did. When we follow His perfect example, we will please God . . . just as Christ did.

Each day, dear Lord, place within my heart a desire to be more like Jesus.

FEBRUARY 19

GOD WILL CARRY YOU

"Blessed are those who mourn, for they shall be comforted."

MATTHEW 5:4

The pain of loss, especially of losing someone we dearly love, can be overwhelming and even incapacitating. Life can bring heartache more painful than we ever thought possible. In those times God can seem distant and even uncaring, but neither is true.

God promises in His Word to be with us always, so no matter what our feelings may suggest, we can *know* that He is with us. He never leaves our side. When our burdens and sorrows seem too heavy for us to bear, He offers to carry them for us, inviting us to cast them upon Him (Psalm 55:22). And when the sorrow is so great that we feel we cannot put one foot in front of the other, God gives us this promise: "I will carry you; I will sustain you" (Isaiah 46:4 NIV).

Lord, when my heart is just too broken, I praise You for Your promise to carry me.

FEBRUARY 20

SEALED WITH THE SPIRIT

Having believed, you were sealed with the Holy Spirit of promise, who is the guarantee of our inheritance.

EPHESIANS 1:13–14

As soon as we become children of God, we are "sealed with His Holy Spirit of promise." This means that the Spirit of God comes to live *inside* us, marking us as true followers of Christ. His presence declares that we are God's own cross-purchased people and that He Himself will watch over us until the day Jesus returns to take us home.

How wonderful to know that God is not ashamed to call us His own; rather He proclaims, *This child belongs to Me!*

But the Holy Spirit is more than a mere marker; He is also our assurance that we will indeed receive our promised inheritance. Not just the mercy and grace God gives us today, but also our eternal home in heaven with Him.

Lord, thank You for Your Spirit and for all the promises He gives me.

FEBRUARY 21

FIND CONTENTMENT

Let your conduct be without covetousness; be content with such things as you have.

HEBREWS 13:5

Contentment is not a popular notion these days. Our culture encourages us to be successful and have lots of possessions.

But the pursuit of toys, fame, and influence can seriously delay the growth and witness of a child of God. Seeking these things can become so all-consuming that the believer forgets his pursuit of God and His way, chasing instead after the temporary comforts of this world's riches. The true wealth of a child of God is his connection with his faithful heavenly Father, who will never abandon him.

Real and lasting contentment is promised to us . . . *if* we surrender our wants and dreams and ambitions to the perfect will of God. We must believe that He is enough, that He will supply all our needs. For where our heart is, there will our treasure be also.

Lord, help me be content with living each moment in Your presence.

FEBRUARY 22

INTO THE PRESENCE

Let us go right into the presence of God with sincere hearts fully trusting him.

HEBREWS 10:22 NLT

Have you ever been to a party or an event to which you weren't really invited? Perhaps you tagged along as a friend of a friend or tried to slip in, only to find yourself face-to-face with the host. It can be uncomfortable!

That never happens with God. He invites us to come "right into the presence." Think on that: the Ruler and Creator of the universe wants to meet with us! Jesus' sacrifice on the cross created this opportunity to step into the presence of God.

The way we act upon God's invitation reveals our hearts' true priorities. He urges us to draw near "with sincere hearts," secure in knowing that we are always invited into His presence.

Lord, what a joy to know I am always welcome in Your presence. Thank You for the invitation.

FEBRUARY 23

ASK AND RECEIVE

"Ask and it will be given to you; seek and you will find; knock and the door will be opened to you."

MATTHEW 7:7 NIV

We are never a bother to God. When we go to Him in prayer, He never thinks, *What now?* When we ask for His blessings in our lives, He doesn't say, *Haven't I given you enough already?* He is a God who loves to give to His people. Not necessarily the things of this world, but rather the spiritual things of His heavenly world—such as goodness and grace, patience and mercy, joy and peace, wisdom and love.

This is great news because we will find, sooner or later, that we cannot live up to His Word without His divine help! He calls us to live as Jesus lived—something we simply cannot do in our own strength. We need His Spirit's insight and guidance. And we need only ask.

Lord, I need Your help to live as Jesus did. I'm asking, seeking, and knocking—and I know You'll answer.

FEBRUARY 24

GOD COMES NEAR

Draw near to God and He will draw near to you.

JAMES 4:8

As with so many of God's promises, it begins with us—something we must first do. In James 4:8, that thing we must do is "draw near to God." Why? Is He not always with us? Yes, God is always with us. The real question is, are we always with Him? Is He ever in our thoughts, in our hearts? Do we turn to Him when troubles come, when blessings come?

In order to draw near to God, we must go to Him often in prayer, believing He hears us. James 4:8 also tells us to "cleanse [our] hands" and "purify [our] hearts"; we do this by telling Him of our sins and trusting Him to forgive us (1 John 1:9). And having done these things, we will have drawn near to God—and He will draw still nearer to us.

Father God, cleanse my heart, my hands, my thoughts so I may step into Your presence.

FEBRUARY 25

BELIEVE AND HAVE LIFE

"He who hears My word and believes in Him who sent Me has everlasting life."

JOHN 5:24

"He who hears My word"—that is the first step toward everlasting life. To listen to and hear the words of Jesus. But that is only the first step. To merely hear is not enough. We must take that next step, or the everlasting life that God so graciously offers will never be ours.

We must go beyond hearing to also believing "in Him who sent Me." Faith in God is the requirement—faith that Jesus came into our world to die in our stead, and that act purchased the forgiveness of our sins. Believing then naturally leads to obeying—for why would we not obey the One in whom we believe?

We have heard the Word, and because we have believed, we are now "most assuredly" (John 5:19) given the "everlasting life" of God's promise.

Open my ears to hear, Lord, my heart to believe, and my hands to obey.

FEBRUARY 26

THE LORD IS STRENGTH

The salvation of the righteous is from the LORD; He is their strength.

PSALM 37:39

The phrase *bone tired* says it well. We can indeed feel physically and emotionally exhausted to the very core, especially when we've been living with difficult and hurtful circumstances.

When you find yourself totally spent, turn to the Lord and let Him fill you with His presence, strengthen your heart, and refresh your spirit. Also ask Him to show you how you reached this point of exhaustion and where, for instance, you may have run ahead of Him or in absolutely the wrong direction. Ask God to help you get on a path of restoration and renewal.

And take Him up on His promise: He is your strength. When you are bone tired, He promises to supply all the help you need.

Lord, I come into Your presence so tired. Let me just rest here with You for a while. Restore and renew me.

FEBRUARY 27

STRENGTH IN TEMPTATION

God is faithful, [He] will not allow you to be temped beyond what you are able, but . . . will also make the way of escape.

1 CORINTHIANS 10:13

Satan tried to tempt even Jesus, and Satan will tempt you. Some temptations will be easily conquered, while others will mean a lengthy and exhausting struggle. Know, however, that God graciously promises to empower you to stand strong against every single temptation you encounter. He also promises to give you a way out of every situation when you are tempted to stray from His path.

What God *doesn't* promise is this: that the choice will be easy. But He also doesn't leave you to withstand temptation by your own strength; instead He encourages you to step boldly before His throne of grace and request His help (Hebrews 4:16). He will give it. When Satan tempts you, you will find the help you need to stand strong. God promises you that.

Lord, I know You are stronger than any temptation the devil can throw at me. Help me stand against him.

FEBRUARY 28

NO FEAR IN LOVE

There is no fear in love; but perfect love casts out fear. . . . We love Him because He first loved us.

1 JOHN 4:18–19

Perfect love casts out fear." Not *our* love for God—because, being human, we can never love faultlessly—but *God's* perfect love for us. That kind of love erases fear.

The love of God is so great, so perfect that He sent a Savior for the world (John 3:16). Our human capacity to love could never be that immense. "For scarcely for a righteous man will one die. . . . But God demonstrates His own love toward us, in that while we were still sinners, Christ died for us" (Romans 5:7–8).

In return, we are able to love because God first loved us. With Him, we need never fear being hurt, rejected, or left alone; His love is unchanging and unending. His flawless love dispels even our deepest fears.

Thank You, Lord, for Your perfect love that leaves me free to love You without reservation or hesitation.

FEBRUARY 29

GOD TEACHES US

Lead me by your truth and teach me, for you are the God who saves me. All day long I put my hope in you.

PSALM 25:5 NLT

In our fast-fix, do-it-yourself, technology-driven society, we can quickly become experts in everything from fixing a leaky faucet to preparing a gourmet soufflé. We're accustomed to having information available with just a few clicks of our fingertips. Waiting for knowledge is not something we're accustomed to doing.

But when it comes to God, we do not develop new character quickly. Yes, His Word is all there for us, but the understanding of it takes time and patience as God slowly peels back the layers of meaning. We learn His ways and His truth gradually as we walk with Him daily. Be patient. God will teach you—the truth and the way to go—but in His own perfect time.

Lord, I eagerly await Your teachings. Open Your Word and Your ways to me.

MARCH

MARCH 1

GOD COMFORTS YOU

Blessed be . . . the Father of mercies and God of all comfort, who comforts us in all our tribulation, that we may be able to comfort those who are in any trouble.

2 CORINTHIANS 1:3–4

The Bible promises that when we seek God, we find Him (Jeremiah 29:13). When we seek His strength, we find it. When we seek His love and peace, His courage and strength, we find it. And when we seek His comfort, we find it.

When we turn to God, our hearts wounded and hurting, longing for the loving embrace of our heavenly Father, He is faithful to deliver. Yes, troubles will come into our lives, but the "God of all comfort" will come too.

And as with so many of His blessings, God's promised gift of comfort is not meant to be hoarded; rather it is to be shared. As He aids us, we learn how to offer reassurance to others. Then when we see those around us hurting and in distress, we are able to reach out, in the love of our Father, and offer comfort.

Father, thank You for the comfort You give me. Help me, in turn, to give to those who need it.

MARCH 2

GOD LEADS US

"I will guide you. . . . Do not be like the horse or like the mule . . . which must be harnessed with bit and bridle."

PSALM 32:8–9

We've all heard the expression "stubborn as a mule," and today's verse warns us about just that. When we allow God to take the reins of our lives, we open ourselves up the wonders of a Spirit-led life. He has promised to instruct us through His Spirit, to teach us the way we should go. Our lessons can be gentle and easy, or they can be more difficult. Much of that depends on our willingness to be taught and led.

We must not be mulish and belligerent, selfishly living for ourselves. Instead, as believers, we should be so aware of the Lord's urgings that He can change our direction with only a nudge. God has promised to show us the way; the method is often up to us.

Lord, forgive me for my stubborn ways. I give the reins of my life to You. Lead me, Lord.

MARCH 3

GOD UPHOLDS US

The steps of a good man are ordered by the Lord, and He delights in his way.

PSALM 37:23

We like to make plans. We ponder them, scribble them on bits of paper, and log them into electronic calendars and checklists. But for all our planning, it is God who ultimately directs our steps (Proverbs 16:9). And for those who love the Lord, it is He who leads them ever closer to Him.

Even the godliest among us will experience dark days and fearful nights. But the Lord will keep us from being destroyed by them. The Lord promises to give us "grace and glory"; indeed, He is "our sun and our shield" (Psalm 84:11 NLT).

We can make plans, but our God's immense love means He is holding tightly to us, teaching us to glorify His name, and ordering our steps all the way home to heaven.

Thank You, Father, for always holding fast to me.

MARCH 4

ANGER THAT FADES

You delight in showing unfailing love.

MICAH 7:18 NLT

Have you ever considered the fact that God owes us nothing? He didn't have to find a way to satisfy His own demand for justice so we could be His for all eternity. He doesn't have to walk with us every day, teaching, enjoying, and guiding us through life.

Why does He do those things? The Lord savors "showing unfailing love." Therefore He maintains faithfulness to us even when we lack faith (2 Timothy 2:13). Before we even knew how destructive sin is, He created a means by which we can be saved from it (Ephesians 1:4). And though we often struggle to hear and follow Him, He stays close at all times (John 10:3).

Who is this God of ours? The God who gives mercy . . . because it delights Him.

Lord, You didn't have to do any of it—not the cross, the tomb, or the resurrection. But I'm so thankful You did.

MARCH 5

GOD'S WORD IS ALIVE

The word of God is living and powerful, and sharper than any two-edged sword.

HEBREWS 4:12

God's Word is alive—and not just alive, but infinitely powerful. It came from the very breath of God (2 Timothy 3:16), and just as that breath breathed life into Adam (Genesis 2:7), it breathes life into His Word. That Book we hold in our hands contains the heart-mending, life-changing, soul-redeeming power of our Lord.

We may make excuses for our disobedience. We may rationalize and justify. We may declare God's Word unreasonable and outdated. And we may even convince ourselves and others that our rebellion against God and His ways really isn't disobedience at all. But God's Word is "sharper than any two-edged sword." It discerns our thoughts and pierces our souls, bringing us into the light of a life lived with Him.

Father, create in me a hunger for Your Word and a burning desire to follow You.

MARCH 6

DESPITE OUR DOUBT

Lord, I believe; help my unbelief!

MARK 9:24

Strong evidence exists for Jesus' resurrection. Science supports creationism. Archaeology unearths relics that support biblical accounts. It's always our choice to believe or not believe.

When we're hurting, though, the choice is especially tough: *Is God hearing my prayers? Does He really care?*

If you find yourself doubting, talk to God about your doubts and open His Word. Notice in Mark 9 that Jesus healed the boy even though his father had doubts. Choose faith—even faith the size of a mustard seed—and God will use it to move mountains (Matthew 17:20). We have the greatest evidence of His existence imaginable: He still works in our lives even when we have doubts.

Lord, I know You're always working in my life for good, but sometimes it's hard to believe. Help my unbelief!

MARCH 7

JESUS FILLS OUR HEARTS

I will praise the Lord *with my whole heart. . . . The* Lord *is gracious and full of compassion.*

PSALM 111:1, 4

Our relationship with Jesus is a matter of the heart. That life-giving relationship has nothing to do with how many times we pray during our waking hours, how many verses (or even chapters!) of the Bible we've memorized, or how much of our paycheck goes into the offering plate.

Our relationship with Jesus is a matter of loving Him with all we are, of making Him most important in our life, of being willing to serve Him instead of doing what we want to do. Our relationship is a matter of having His Spirit show us our sin and then confessing that sin to Him so that being forgiven, we can enjoy our friendship with Jesus. And so He can once again completely fill our hearts.

Lord Jesus, I know I can do nothing to make You love me more . . . or less. I come now just to rest in Your love.

MARCH 8

NO CONDEMNATION

There is therefore now no condemnation to those who are in Christ Jesus, who do not walk according to the flesh, but according to the Spirit.

ROMANS 8:1

We can walk one of two ways through this life: according to the flesh or according to the Spirit. Walking according to the flesh subjects us to sin and pain. But walking according to the Spirit, by submitting our lives to God, frees us from sin and pain.

Continuing in the ways of the flesh is a bit like taking a journey with a heavy load strapped to your back. At first, it might not seem so burdensome. But with each step, it grows heavier, pulling you down.

When you choose to walk with the Holy Spirit, He not only lifts that heavy load, He also lifts *you* up on the wings of the risen Lord Jesus—allowing you to soar above the ways of this world.

Father, open my heart to the leading of the Holy Spirit, so I may soar above the ways of the world.

MARCH 9

COMING BACK

The Lord Himself will descend from heaven with a shout, with the voice of an archangel, and with the trumpet of God.

1 THESSALONIANS 4:16

The Son of Man will come upon the clouds with the trumpet of God heralding His arrival. Just imagine all the saints rising up together to meet Him in the air (1 Thessalonians 4:17). On that day, every knee will bow and every tongue will confess that Jesus is Lord (Philippians 2:10–11).

If skeptics struggle to believe that God created all the wonders of our world—when so much evidence is right before their eyes—what must they think of the promise of Jesus' return? When the sun and moon will be darkened, the stars will fall, and "the powers in the heavens will be shaken" (Mark 13:24–26)?

But amid all the glories we'll witness, let's not lose sight of the promise, the true reason for the moment: Jesus is returning, and He is coming to carry us home.

Lord, whatever troubles this world holds, I cling to the promise that You will come and take me home.

MARCH 10

EASE THE ACHE

I cried to the LORD with my voice, and He heard me. . . . I will not be afraid . . . of people who have set themselves against me.

PSALM 3:4, 6

Perhaps nothing is as devastating as being betrayed by someone you love and trust. Know that Jesus—betrayed by Judas, denied by Peter—fully understands. He will enable you to recover. The key, as hard as it is, is to pray for that person and ask God to bless him or her.

When you pray to God—and you may have to do this again and again—you release the anger and disappointment that come with being betrayed. It is difficult to despise someone you lift up in prayer. And though retaliating is a natural response, it's not a godly one. Praying is always the best option. Allow the Lord to receive your hurt and to replace it with His peace.

Lord, I release my anger and pain to You. Free me from bad feelings and empower me to love.

MARCH 11

FILLED WITH JOY

Though now you do not see Him, yet believing,
you rejoice with joy inexpressible.

1 PETER 1:8

Did you know that God offers you deep-down, bubbling-over joy? As you are committed to Christ, dedicated to service, reverent and holy, you can also be filled with inexpressible joy. That is possible because of this wonderful truth: we are loved by the Lord perfectly and completely.

We've all heard that Christian joy exists apart from what is happening in our daily lives; it exists because of Christ our risen Savior. But it is also dependent upon us, upon our choosing to embrace the joy of His love, choosing to think on things that are good and pure, lovely and noble (Philippians 4:8).

God will give His children joy, but as with all the gifts of God, we must be willing to reach out and accept it.

Lord, I cannot count the number of reasons You have given me to be joyful—but help me to try each day.

MARCH 12

STILLING THE STORM

We have peace with God through our Lord Jesus Christ.

ROMANS 5:1

When we place our faith in Christ, the stormy seas of our lives—churned up by our own sins—are stilled. And while the storms may still rage *around* us in this sin-plagued world, they do not rage *within* us. That does not mean our troubles and tribulations are over, but it does mean we can rest in knowing God will see us through them. Think about how Jesus dealt with the storm that threatened to sink the boat: "He arose and rebuked the winds and the sea, and there was a great calm" (Matthew 8:26).

God is ever at work in the lives of His children. While no one enjoys the stormy and difficult times, we can be assured that we never battle in vain. God will use those times for our benefit. And He will give us the peace we need to persevere.

Thank You, God, for sending Jesus, so I have a way to find Your peace in the storms.

MARCH 13

GOD WILL ANSWER

"Whatever things you ask in prayer, believing, you will receive."

MATTHEW 21:22

Has it ever seemed that God was slow to answer your prayers? Or perhaps wasn't answering at all? The truth is that God *does* answer every prayer. And when our prayers are inspired by His Spirit, God always gives us what we ask for—or something better.

How can we know our prayers are inspired? As we surrender our wills to the Lord's, even those prayers that began outside His will are turned to it by the work of His Spirit. Just listen to this reassuring promise: "The Spirit . . . helps in our weaknesses. For we do not know what we should pray for as we ought, but the Spirit Himself makes intercession for us" (Romans 8:26). Keep praying, keep surrendering, and by "believing, you will receive."

Lord, I know that every time I pray, You listen and answer. Help me rest in Your perfect care.

MARCH 14

WE HAVE PURPOSE

We are His workmanship, created in Christ Jesus for good works, which God prepared beforehand that we should walk in them.

EPHESIANS 2:10

We can sing and shout and share the praises of God for His gift of salvation. But we are never to boast in it (Ephesians 2:8–9). We did not earn our place in heaven, and we can never deserve it. When we respond to God's offer of salvation, He delivers to us a pure and unimaginable gift.

But our generous God does not stop with salvation or even a heavenly inheritance. He also gifts us with a purpose and a calling. "We are His workmanship"—He created us to do a job, to do good works—and He already has them all planned out for us. Each is as unique as the individual He calls to do it. But we are united in this: our purpose, our calling is to draw others to Him. When we give our lives to God's work, our lives praise Him.

Thank You, Lord, for salvation and for giving me a purpose, a chance to praise You through the good things I do.

MARCH 15

GOOD GIFTS

Every good gift and every perfect gift is from above, and comes down from the Father of lights.

JAMES 1:17

Take a moment to look around you. What do you see? People you love? Work you're skilled at? Are you able to rise up in the morning? Do you have enough to share with others? Do you have something to smile about? These are all things given you from the hand of God.

Do you also have love and joy, peace and patience, strength and courage, mercy and grace? Do you have salvation and the hope of a heavenly home? These are God's greatest gifts.

God graciously lavishes His goodness upon His children. His gifts are perfect. And just as we do not boast in our salvation because it is the work of God, we should not boast in the blessings we've been given. Rather we should praise God, for every good and perfect gift comes from Him.

Lord, of the gifts You give me, I thank You most of all for Your perfect love.

MARCH 16

YOUR STRENGTH

The Lord is the strength of my life; of whom shall I be afraid?

PSALM 27:1

In Psalm 27, David unashamedly proclaimed that the Lord was the strength of his life. And then he went further and dared to ask, "Of whom shall I be afraid?"

Can we not do the same? Can we not claim God's promised strength for our own? Can we not declare that with God by our side, no one can make us tremble in fear? Yes, we can! We need not fear the darkness, because God is our light. We need not fear the enemy, because God is our salvation (v. 1). He shelters us (v. 5), lifts us up (v. 6), teaches us the way we should go (v. 11), and shows us His goodness (v. 13).

David was right: the Lord is our strength for life.

Lord, I do not fear the things of this life, because I am Yours. I rest in Your presence and protection.

MARCH 17

GOD REWARDS SERVANTS

"His lord said to him, 'Well done, good and faithful servant. . . . Enter into the joy of your lord.'"

MATTHEW 25:21

The parable of the talents found in Matthew 25 offers us both a lesson and a promise. The lesson is that we have each been given a unique gift, and along with that gift comes a responsibility to use it for God's glory.

But there is at least one gift that all believers share: the love of Jesus. And our lives should reflect that love into the world. It must shine through our words and our actions so that others see not us, but Him.

This parable is also God's promise to reward us when we faithfully use the gifts we've been given. Our reward is an everlasting crown of righteousness (2 Timothy 4:8). It is living for eternity in the holy presence of God. It is hearing the words, "Well done, good and faithful servant."

Lord, give me the courage to use the gifts You've given me, so that one day I'll hear You say, "Well done."

MARCH 18

DEATH'S DEFEAT

If we died with Christ, we believe that we shall also live with Him, knowing that Christ, having been raised from the dead, dies no more.

ROMANS 6:8–9

When we surrendered our selfish ways and chose to follow Jesus rather than the world, we also chose to die to the ways of sin and to begin a new life in Christ.

That choice is possible because Jesus' work on the cross erased sin's ownership of us. He was the perfect, spotless Lamb, so His sacrifice was sufficient to cover all our sins (1 Peter 3:18). Because Jesus died for our sins, we don't have to.

But Jesus didn't settle for simply erasing our sins. When He rose up out of the tomb on that third day, He declared death's defeat. The grave no longer rules us. Because Jesus lives, we too can live. Not in the old ways of this world, but in a new life with Christ.

Jesus, You shattered the power of sin and death—and You did it for me. Thank You, Lord, for a love so great.

MARCH 19

GOD IS ABLE

To Him who is able to do exceedingly abundantly above all that we ask or think, according to the power that works in us, to Him be glory.

EPHESIANS 3:20–21

When we pray, God answers. But God's answers are not always what we expect.

Sometimes God answers no when we expect a yes. Sometimes He says yes when deep inside we're expecting a no. And sometimes God says yes in a way that is "infinitely beyond our greatest prayers, hopes, or dreams" (Ephesians 3:20 AMP). Why? Because God is able, and because He delights in giving His children good gifts (Matthew 7:11).

God is able to love us when we are unlovable. He is able to carry out His perfect purpose in our imperfect lives. He is able to shield and strengthen us. And He will do this until we arrive in heaven.

God gives a promise to those who faithfully follow Him: when we pray, He answers—abundantly.

Father, I will trust You to answer my prayers—
and I cannot wait to see what You do!

MARCH 20

GOD'S TREASURE

"They shall be Mine," says the Lord of hosts, "on the day that I make them My jewels."

MALACHI 3:17

The pearl of great price. Jesus told the story about the merchant who sold all that he had to purchase that one special pearl. It was a parable meaning we should be willing to give up all we have in order to gain the treasure of heaven (Matthew 13:45–46).

But have you ever considered that God sees each of us as a pearl, a precious jewel? And He paid a great price to purchase us for His kingdom—the sacrifice of His Son. Having purchased us, God treasures and adores us. He claims us as His own and opens up the gates of heaven to us.

We are God's jewels, His pearls of great price. Therefore let us celebrate every day the wondrous love of our Father—and the joyful truth that we belong to Him.

Father, it's hard to imagine You count me as one of Your treasures, but I'm so very glad You do!

MARCH 21

IN OUR MIDST

"Where two or three are gathered together in My name, I am there in the midst of them."

MATTHEW 18:20

How many times have we attended meetings when the key person involved didn't show up? Or was late? Or he came, but he completely ignored everyone and fiddled with his phone the whole time?

It's not only annoying and unproductive; it's also hurtful. The message received is loud and clear: *you aren't worth my time or my attention.*

Now consider this: when two or more gather in Jesus' name to worship and pray—when we call a meeting of the faithful—Jesus promises to be there with us, in our midst. He shows up, right on time, giving us His full attention. And the message He sends is loud and clear: *You are important to Me; you are worth My time and attention. Here I am with you.*

Jesus, how amazing and how comforting to know that when I gather with other believers, You gather with us.

MARCH 22

HOME WITH US

"If anyone loves Me, he will keep My word; and My Father will love him, and We will come to him and make Our home with him."

JOHN 14:23

Home. What images, what emotions does that word call to mind? A warm fireplace on a cold night. Joyful laughter around the kitchen table. A safe place to rest, renew, and recharge. A place of love and peace.

Jesus offers us a home—and not just the someday home of heaven. But a home with Him, in His presence, here and now. Jesus said, "If anyone loves Me, he will keep My word." And from our love and obedience springs a promise: if we keep His word, obey Him, He and God will make their home with us. His Holy Spirit will come to live *within* us. In this home with and of God, we will find a safe place to rest, renew, and recharge. A place of warmth and peace and love. A home with God.

Jesus, I do love You. Make Your home with me so I might live each day in Your presence.

MARCH 23

TRANSFORMED MIND

Do not be conformed to this world, but be transformed by the renewing of your mind, that you may prove what is that good and acceptable and perfect will of God.

ROMANS 12:2

If we are not careful, we will be molded and shaped by the world around us, conformed to its standards—or lack thereof. A little drop of our guard here, a little loosening of our standards there, and soon we will find ourselves indistinguishable from the world around us.

That is why Paul urges us in Romans 12:1 to present ourselves to God as a living sacrifice; to relinquish our own desires to the service of God. And that sacrifice begins with our minds—not only what we allow ourselves to think, but also what we allow into our minds. When we surrender our thoughts and our wills to God, He is faithful to renew and transform our minds, filling our thoughts with His "good and acceptable and perfect will."

Lord, I surrender my thoughts to You. Guide me to those things that are good and acceptable.

MARCH 24

PERFECT PEACE

You will keep him in perfect peace, whose mind is stayed on You, because he trusts in You.

ISAIAH 26:3

Within each of us lies an innate desire for true and lasting, perfect peace. We try all sorts of things to find it—yoga, meditation, relaxation. None of those things are wrong, in and of themselves, but they are not the source of truc and perfect peace. Only One can give that sort of peace: God.

Making God the center of our thoughts—keeping our minds "stayed on" Him—naturally leads to His also becoming the center of our words, our actions, and our emotions. When we trust in Him, we believe that He is in control, that He is strong enough to do whatever needs to be done, and that He is loving enough to ensure His best for us. Worries and doubts and fears flee before Him, leaving us with His promised perfect peace.

Lord, keep my wandering thoughts focused on You, and please fill me with Your perfect peace.

MARCH 25

HIS SPIRIT GIVES LIFE

"It is the Spirit who gives life; the flesh profits nothing."

JOHN 6:63

So many people during Jesus' time on earth could not see past the literal and physical that was right in front of their eyes. The religious leaders particularly struggled with this, but so did His own disciples at times. In John 6:54, when Jesus said, "Whoever eats My flesh and drinks My blood has eternal life," He was speaking symbolically of His coming sacrifice. But many could not get past the literal meaning of His words.

This led Jesus to explain in verse 63 that "human effort accomplishes nothing" (NLT). It is not literal bread and wine that give life; it is only the Spirit of God who gives eternal life. And that eternal life is promised to those who believe the words of Jesus and choose to partake of the "bread" of His life.

Lord, help me look beyond the physical world right in front of me. Show me the true meaning of Your words.

MARCH 26

OUR GOOD SHEPHERD

"I am the good shepherd; and I know My sheep, and am known by My own."

JOHN 10:14

A shepherd watches over his sheep. Just as there are good sheep and bad sheep, there are also good shepherds and bad ones. In John 10, Jesus declared that He is not just *a* good shepherd, but Hc is *the* Good Shepherd.

"I know My sheep," He says. We are *known by Jesus*! We aren't just random bits of fleece wandering around in His pasture. He knows us, hearts and souls, and calls us by name (John 10:3).

Jesus not only knows His sheep, but He is known by His sheep. We recognize His voice, because we have spent time with Him and have learned the words He speaks. As our Shepherd, He guides us, shields us, and provides for us. He searches for us when we wander away. Jesus lays down His life for the sheep (v. 15). He is the Good Shepherd.

Lord, I am so thankful to be part of Your flock.

MARCH 27

EVERLASTING WORD

"Heaven and earth will pass away, but My words will by no means pass away."

LUKE 21:33

So many things these days don't last as long as they used to—cars, appliances, even many relationships. But the Word of God lasts forever. One day "heaven and earth will pass away," at least as we now know them, but God's words "will by no means pass away."

How important is God's promise that His Word never changes, that it is eternal? In a world where every other answer changes, it is the very foundation of our lives of faith. His Word is the source of perfect wisdom—the very words of the Lord our God Himself. Within its Spirit-inspired pages are the answers to every dilemma, every quandary, every struggle we will ever face.

Open God's Word, and let it fill you with His truth today.

Father, I am so grateful for Your Word—that I can go to it anytime, anywhere to hear Your voice and seek Your face.

MARCH 28

OUR ADVOCATE

If anyone sins, we have an Advocate with the Father, Jesus Christ the righteous. And He Himself is the propitiation for our sins.

1 JOHN 2:1–2

Take a moment to reread today's verses. Did you see it? It's such an amazing promise: "If anyone sins, we have an Advocate with the Father."

Just as Abraham stood before God and pleaded for Lot and the sin-filled cities of Sodom and Gomorrah, just as Moses stood before God and pleaded for the stiff-necked Israelites, so Jesus stands before our Lord and pleads for us. Jesus asks the Father to accept His sacrifice instead of requiring ours. Jesus Himself pays the price for our sins.

If you've ever had anyone stand up to defend you, you know the joy of having an Advocate like Jesus. And if you've ever had anyone say, "I'll pay the debt he owes," you have a sense of the overwhelming gratitude we all owe our Savior.

Thank You, Father, for Your Son. And thank You, Jesus, for the payment You made for my sins.

MARCH 29

JESUS BREAKS WALLS

[Jesus] Himself is our peace, who has made both one, and has broken down the middle wall of separation.

EPHESIANS 2:14

For so many years, Jews and Gentiles were separated by a wall of tradition and religion. But Jesus came and broke down that wall. A Jewish person who believes Jesus is the Son of God gains a new identity, as does a believing Gentile: they are now both "in Christ." Where once there was a wall of separation, there is now unity in spirit—they are made one.

Are there other walls that separate people? Walls of tradition or religion, of race or economics? We were created to be one in Christ. When we truly surrender ourselves to His love, His will, and His way, Jesus will shatter any barriers between us.

Father, help me fully surrender my life to You so any walls I've built will come crashing down.

MARCH 30

YOU HAVE FAVOR

Let not mercy and truth forsake you; . . . and so find favor and high esteem in the sight of God and man.

PROVERBS 3:3–4

When we call ourselves Christians, the way we live each day reflects on our Lord. The question we must then continually ask ourselves is this: *Is it an accurate reflection?* Do our lives demonstrate the love, mercy, and grace of our God—and thereby please Him? Or do they reflect the world—and disappoint the One who has done so much for us?

Just as God offers mercy and truth to us, so we should offer them to all who cross our paths. But remember, mercy and truth must go hand in hand. For truth alone can create heartless rule-keeping, while mercy alone can cause us to accept that which God has declared unacceptable. It's only when *both* mercy and truth are offered, through love, that we demonstrate the true nature of God—and thus enjoy His favor.

Father, may my life always reflect
Your mercy and truth and love.

MARCH 31

ABIDE WITH GOD

If anyone loves the world, the love of the Father is not in him. . . . But he who does the will of God abides forever.

1 JOHN 2:15, 17

Many in this world are hostile to God. Some in our society revel in serving their own self-centeredness, wayward desires, and quests for power and fame. But such things are pursuits for the worldly, not the believer.

When we seek to satisfy the flesh, earthly belongings and influences offer only temporary happiness. We will never find true and lasting fulfillment in those things because they do not come from the Father. Only in Him can we find what truly fills us up and makes us whole.

As His children, we do not live for those things that wither like the grass and fall away (1 Peter 1:24). Instead we live for God. And because we choose His ways over the world's, He gifts us with life forever with Him.

Lord, help me not to be caught up in worldly pleasures. Protect me from the evil one's temptations.

APRIL

APRIL 1

GRACIOUS SALVATION

Put all your hope in the gracious salvation that will come to you when Jesus Christ is revealed to the world.

1 PETER 1:13 NLT

Just as God who calls us is holy, so we also are to be holy in all we do and say and think (v. 15). That's not a task to take lightly. To see godly change in our daily living requires purposeful, determined changes of habit and thought.

But keep in mind that holiness is not a joyless pursuit of religious activity void of fun and pleasure. Nehemiah wrote, "The joy of the LORD is your strength" (8:10); therefore, it is God the Father who gives us the power to live delight-filled lives.

Don't miss out on all the joyful moments God sprinkles into your life—yes, even amid the struggles and troubles. Seek Him first (Matthew 6:33), and set your hope on "the gracious salvation" you will receive when Jesus comes again. That will inspire a holy happiness that floods into others' lives.

Father, help me find the joy of serving You. And let that joy so shine that others will want to follow You too.

APRIL 2

COMPLETE IN CHRIST

In Him dwells all the fullness of the Godhead bodily; and you are complete in Him.

COLOSSIANS 2:9–10

God's Word teaches us a deep truth: Jesus was both completely human and completely God at the same time. To know God better, watch and listen to Jesus. He gives us a full and beautiful picture of who our Father is.

But now consider this fact: "all the fullness of the Godhead" is present in the Son. That means all the power to forgive, to love, to offer grace and mercy and salvation is found in Christ. When we become followers of Christ, we receive all the blessings of that power. We are given everything we need to live godly lives As Jesus said, "No one comes to the Father except through Me" (John 14:6). Nothing else is needed. Totally human and totally divine, Christ makes us complete.

Jesus, You fill in all the empty spaces and make me whole. Thank You for supplying all I need.

APRIL 3

CHILDREN OF GOD

As many as received Him, to them He gave the right to become children of God.

JOHN 1:12

God chose the Jewish nation as His people millennia ago. Yet the Jews were the first to reject Jesus as the promised Messiah. God's chosen did not recognize God's only begotten (v. 11).

So Jesus then made salvation available through His blood to everyone. Not just to the devout, the moral, the upright, but to anyone who saw the need for a Savior from sin. And while many disregarded Him, some did not, and to those He gave the privilege of becoming God's own children. When we choose Jesus, we get to become part of God's family. Not because of Abraham or our ancestors, not because we do all the "right" things or are especially religious. We receive His promised adoption because we choose to believe He truly is the Son of God.

Jesus, I believe You are the Holy One who came to offer me salvation. Thank You!

APRIL 4

THE LORD'S BEAUTY

Let the beauty of the LORD our God be upon us,
and establish the work of our hands.

PSALM 90:17

The beauty of the Lord. It truly is always within sight, if we have a heart willing to seek it and eyes open to see it.

Yes, there's the obvious beauty of God's creation. The soaring mountains, gloriously green valleys, and thundering seas. And there's the less-tangible beauty of a mother's sacrificial love, a father's guiding presence, a friend's loyalty to lean upon.

But then there is also the unexpected beauty of a Savior nailed to a cross. For the believer, this image represents the greatest beauty of all: Mercy, as we are spared the punishment we deserve. Grace, as we receive all the blessings we could never earn. It is God's beautiful love at work.

May the Lord ever shine His beauty upon us.

Father, open my eyes to see Your loveliness in all its many shapes and forms and ways.

APRIL 5

WALK IN LIGHT

If we walk in the light as He is in the light, we have fellowship with one another, and the blood of Jesus Christ His Son cleanses us from all sin.

1 JOHN 1:7

If we walk in the light, practicing obedience, we can know God and have fellowship with Him. God does not demand or even expect perfection; He knows we're human. What He does demand are people who *seek* to obey Him in all things, even as we do so imperfectly. With that kind of life, God can establish a relationship with us that will guide us ever closer to Him—and will pull us back to Him—if and when we disobey.

And then there's an additional blessing: "we have fellowship with one another." Walking in the light produces harmony and companionship. When we walk faithfully with God, we walk happily with fellow believers. Obedience brings many rewards.

Father, help me seek obedience to You in all things. Guide me in the way I should go.

APRIL 6

GOD WILL HELP

"Fear not, for I am with you. . . . I will strengthen you, yes, I will help you, I will uphold you with My righteous right hand."

ISAIAH 41:10

All of us confront fearful situations at times; it's part of living in this fallen world. The real question for us is this: How will we handle that fear when it comes? Will we fall back on the advice and remedies and fast fixes of this world? Or will we remember that we are children of God—and claim the promises that belong to us?

As kinfolk of God, we are promised that God is always with us. When we trust Him, when we look to Him for guidance, He gives us His courage and strength. God helps His children. Never feel foolish about your faith, especially in times of fear. Instead, put God first in your life—He promises to uphold you with His "righteous right hand."

Father, I know I cannot escape this world's troubles. But I also know You will strengthen and help me.

APRIL 7

THE SPIRIT'S TEMPLE

Do you not know that your body is the temple of the Holy Spirit . . . and you are not your own? For you were bought at a price.

1 CORINTHIANS 6:19–20

How precious is your body? Do you take it for granted, assuming it will always serve you as you need it to? Do you honor its needs with nutritious food and regular exercise? If you find these questions a bit direct and personal, you might respond, "My personal health is my business."

The fact is, "you were bought at a price" by Jesus, who gave His own body to be slain on our behalf. If we harm or misuse our bodies, we are no better than vandals, desecrating that which doesn't belong to us.

But because we belong to God, we are blessed with this beautiful promise: our bodies are "the temple of the Holy Spirit." We are the home of God's own Spirit! Let's make it a home worthy of Him by treating our bodies as the treasure they are.

Lord, I belong to You. Use me to honor You.

APRIL 8

BELIEVING = RIGHTEOUS

Because of Abraham's faith, God counted him as righteous.

ROMANS 4:22 NLT

Do you have the faith of Abraham? Could you, like the Israelite patriarch, believe God's promise though *decades* pass before it is fulfilled? It was *twenty-five years* before the son God promised the old couple appeared (Genesis 12:4; 17:15–17). *Twenty-five years* before God made the impossible possible.

Yet through all those barren years, Abraham continued to believe, and "it was accounted to him for righteousness."

God cannot lie. He will never put His guarantee on something He can't provide. Do we really believe that? If we claim to believe it, do our lives show it? Do we trust Him no matter how illogical it may seem? God's promises are unwavering. Believe in Him. Let your life reflect that belief . . . and it will be credited to you as righteousness.

Father, with everything I do and say, help me live out my trust in You and Your promises.

APRIL 9

HIS KINDNESS IS FOREVER

How abundant are the good things that you have stored up for those who fear you.

PSALM 31:19 NIV

When we think of the great promises of God, we usually think of His gifts of salvation, mercy, and the forgiveness of sins. We consider our future heavenly home, our gathering with loved ones in the hereafter, an eternity of bliss. But how often do we think of the *kindness* of the Lord?

God could have simply saved us from His wrath, given us a home in heaven, and declared Himself done. But He did not. God walks with us each day, watches over us each night, knows each hair on our heads and engraves our names upon His own hand as proof we are never out of His thoughts. Because of His covenant with us, He sends sunshine and rain, laughter and joy—not because He has to, but because God loves being kind to those who call Him Lord.

Lord, help me offer kindness to all who cross my path.

APRIL 10

IT PLEASES OUR FATHER

It pleased the Father . . . to reconcile all things to Himself.

COLOSSIANS 1:19–20

"It pleased the Father." There are many beautiful promises centered around our reconciliation to God—the mercy, the grace, the cleansing of our souls, the place prepared for us in heaven. But perhaps the most breathtakingly beautiful thing about the reconciliation promises is the reason behind them: "It pleased the Father."

In Isaiah, the Lord said it this way: "I, even I, am He who blots out your transgressions for My own sake" (43:25). Don't underestimate the power of this simple statement. The Lord God—*El Shaddai*, *Jehovah*, *Yahweh*—washes away our transgressions for His own sake, because it pleases Him to do so. God does so much for us, blesses us with so many promises, but it's this glimpse into His *why* that should make our hearts sing with joy.

Lord Jesus, I'll never understand the true depth of Your love, but I am so very grateful that it includes me.

APRIL 11

NEVER ALONE

"I will not leave you orphans; I will come to you."

JOHN 14:18

Being alone—especially when the days are dark, when the troubles are many, when our world is overwhelming—can be a frightening thing. Perhaps that's why this promise of Jesus is the source of such comfort and strength: "I will not leave you orphans; I will come to you."

Jesus will never leave us all alone. Once we choose to become His followers, His children, we will never experience His abandonment, His being distracted, His forgetting our problems. He's the Friend above all friends.

Savor the joy of that promise: He comes to us via the Spirit of God. He makes His home within us so He is always close. He comes to guide, to teach, to intercede, to reveal. But He also comes simply to *be* with us, our Comforter and constant Companion. We are never left alone.

Lord, when I am feeling lonely, stir Your Spirit within me; comfort me with Your constant presence.

APRIL 12

OUR SINS ARE GONE

As far as the east is from the west, so far has He removed our transgressions from us.

PSALM 103:12

It's not surprising that God is a geographical genius. After all, He created geography. Psalm 103:12 says that our sins are removed from us "as far as the east is from the west." Notice that God says "east" and "west," not "north" and "south." That is because if you start traveling north around the globe, eventually you'll crest over the top and find yourself going south. But east will never meet west. You can travel west until the end of time and never be headed east.

Why does that matter? Because that is how far God has removed our sins from us. Just as east and west will never meet, so the believer and his sins will never again meet.

Father, thank You for setting my sins so far away from me. Your mercies amaze me.

APRIL 13

HEIRS OF GOD

The Spirit Himself bears witness with our spirit that we are children of God, and if children, then heirs—heirs of God and joint heirs with Christ.

ROMANS 8:16–17

Children of God. That is what we become when we choose to believe, to follow, and to obey Jesus. The Word tells us this is true: "Behold what manner of love the Father has bestowed on us, that we should be called children of God!" (1 John 3:1). "The Spirit Himself bears witness" and whispers to our hearts that we do indeed belong to God.

What does that mean exactly? It means we are siblings with Christ. Membership in His family brings gifts and honors we can barely comprehend. As coheirs with Christ, we will inherit the family kingdom! And beyond the divine inheritance, we receive the riches of our daily inheritance—the Father's great love for His children.

Lord, today I praise You for the daily inheritance of Your love.

APRIL 14

JESUS OVERCOMES ALL

"In the world you will have tribulation; but be of good cheer, I have overcome the world."

JOHN 16:33

Jesus knew that not long after He spoke these words He would be arrested, tried, and crucified. He knew the disciples would run away and hide. He knew Peter would deny Him. But Jesus also knew He would not be alone; His Father would be with Him.

Even knowing their betrayal was coming, Jesus was concerned for His disciples. He knew they would soon be confronted, ridiculed, beaten, and even murdered. But Jesus also knew that since the cross was coming, sin and death would be defeated. And the Spirit was coming—He would strengthen and sustain His disciples no matter what the world threw at them. That's how Jesus could say, "Be of good cheer." Because He knew He would overcome all that was coming. And because He did, we can too.

Lord, You overcame all the troubles and temptations of this world. Help me overcome them too.

APRIL 15

HE CHOOSES YOU

Has God not chosen the poor of this world to be rich in faith and heirs of the kingdom which He promised to those who love Him?

JAMES 2:5

In the divine economy of God, "poverty" has little to do with our paychecks. Rather in God's eyes, to be "poor in spirit" (Matthew 5:3) is to know that we cannot "do" this life without God. No amount of wealth or power will get us into heaven.

So often worldly poverty is equated with spiritual riches. But worldly riches do not preclude a person from God's kingdom. Abraham was righteous—and rich. David was a man after God's own heart—and his kingly accounts were quite full. The trouble with earthly riches is that they tend to distract us from God and turn our focus to our bank accounts. But when we center our lives on loving God, we are promised all the spiritual wealth of His kingdom—no matter how rich or poor we are.

Lord, let me not depend on the wealth of this world but rather turn to You as my greatest treasure.

APRIL 16

FIRST THINGS FIRST

"Seek the kingdom of God, and all these things shall be added to you."

LUKE 12:31

Food, clothing, shelter—these are the things we need in this world. But so often we get caught up in chasing after the "good" food, the "right" clothes, the "better-than-the Joneses'" houses. We care more about what others think of us and our stuff than what Jesus thinks of our souls.

Jesus tells us to first "seek the kingdom of God," and then everything else will fall into place. Consider those first disciples Jesus commissioned to tell the world about Him. They may have appeared ordinary, yet they were rich in their faith. As followers of Christ, we can be too. There's no need to worry about the daily needs of life. When we seek Christ and His ways, He takes care of the rest.

Father, the daily grind so easily tears my focus from You. Remind me that You will take care of all my needs.

APRIL 17

THE LAW OF THE LORD

His delight is in the law of the Lord, and in His law he meditates day and night. He shall be like a tree planted by the rivers of water . . . and whatever he does shall prosper.

PSALM 1:2–3

Obedience is a sure path to the heart of God. He delights in seeing His children find holy and right ways of living and then enjoy all the benefits of a righteous life. And while it's true that even the obedient face challenges, they also find delight in the Lord's blessings. As the psalmist wrote, they will flourish like well-watered trees.

But how do we know *how* to obey Him? We begin with meditating on His Word, finding delight in His commandments, and then following them. It is just impossible to truly love and please God without also loving His revealed words.

When we find our delight in heeding the "law of the Lord," God delights in blessing us so that whatever we do shall prosper.

Lord, open my eyes to the beauty and truth of Your Word so I shall be like a tree planted by the waters.

APRIL 18

PERFECT INSTRUCTIONS

The instructions of the Lord are perfect, reviving the soul.

PSALM 19:7 NLT

Psalm 19 tells us of the perfection of the natural world God created: "the heavens declare the glory of God" (v. 1). It also tells us that the sun "bursts forth like a radiant bridegroom after his wedding" (v. 5 NLT) and that His laws are "more desirable than gold" (v. 10 NLT). All this is possible because God Himself is full of power and glory.

When we need the strength and courage to face a difficult day, we can turn to this psalm. It is our prayer for God's flawless wisdom and guidance, because the God who created birds, flowers, mountains, galaxies, field mice, and you and me also offers us His guidance for daily living. And surely the One who has "set a tabernacle for the sun" (v. 4) can handle any problem we might face. For His instructions are no less than "perfect"!

Lord, I turn to You not only in times of trouble, but in each day of my life.

APRIL 19

SURRENDER

"I will give you a new heart and put a new spirit within you; I will take the heart of stone out of your flesh and give you a heart of flesh."

EZEKIEL 36:26

Have you ever thought about what it means to completely surrender yourself to God? The word *surrender* suggests not having control over your life, and it can sound scary. But when you give yourself to God, His blessings will flow into your life.

Choose to surrender your thoughts to God. Choose to praise Him, open your Bible, or pray. And on those days you struggle to surrender, remember that it is not a once-and-done event. It is an ongoing process that God uses to transform you into the image of His Son (Romans 12:1–2).

Surrendering yourself—your heart, your thoughts, every minute of your day—to God is your choice. It's a choice God will help you live out. And it's a choice He will bless.

Lord, on those days when I struggle to let You take control, remind me of Your faithful goodness.

APRIL 20

REAP WHAT YOU SOW

He who sows sparingly will also reap sparingly, and he who sows bountifully will also reap bountifully.

2 CORINTHIANS 9:6

Some promises are for blessings; others are for consequences. The words of 2 Corinthians 9:6 are both. And though they are often applied to money, they go far beyond that.

When we give love, we will get love. When we give kindness and compassion, we will receive kindness and compassion. And yes, when it comes to material things, when we give to help those around us, God will make sure we do not go without.

The reverse is also true. If we are stingy with our love, kindness, and compassion, we cannot expect others to extend those things to us. If we see someone in need and do not help, we cannot expect God to bless us.

Give, and give cheerfully. Then God will make sure that you "reap bountifully."

Lord, thank You for Your many blessings. Show me ways to share them with others.

APRIL 21

THE LAMB WILL LEAD

The Lamb who is in the midst of the throne will shepherd them and lead them to living fountains of waters.

REVELATION 7:17

Jesus is the Lamb who sacrificed Himself to save us. For now, here on earth, we see and hear Him through His Word and through the gentle nudgings of His Holy Spirit. But one day, when we join Him in heaven, we will see our precious Lamb face to wondrous face. He will stretch out His hand to enfold ours. We will hear Him say, "Follow Me," and He will lead us to "living fountains of waters."

Never again will we thirst for His Word, for His voice will be forever in our ears. Never again will we hunger for His presence, for He will be right by our sides. No more tears, no sorrows, no sadness, no pain. Only the joyous perfection of an eternity with the Lamb.

The Lamb will lead those who belong to Him.

Jesus, knowing that one day I will look into Your face fills me with such joy. Lead me home to heaven with You.

APRIL 22

THE LONG-SUFFERING LORD

The Lord is not slack concerning His promise . . . but is longsuffering toward us, not willing that any should perish.

2 PETER 3:9

Our God is full of loving-kindness and patience. Why do you think He tarries in retrieving His people from this godless, destructive world? Because He wants one more soul, and then another, to be saved. God doesn't measure time the way we do, with our calendars and schedules. He is infinite and unlimited by the finite.

God wants every person to be His own—even those we think couldn't possibly get into heaven. He longs for an enormous family of children. While we feel impatient for His coming, He feels yearning for the lost sons and daughters of men. And while we may get frustrated with God's longsuffering toward some, aren't we so very grateful that He patiently waits for those lost ones we love?

Lord, I pray that all would come to know you,
and I especially pray now for . . .

APRIL 23

JESUS UNDERSTANDS

We do not have a High Priest who cannot sympathize with our weaknesses, but was in all points tempted as we are, yet without sin.

HEBREWS 4:15

Jesus knows the pull and power of temptation. He has felt the sting of longing, whether it was for food, rest, or escape from pain. Therefore when we face temptation, we have a Friend who has been where we are. He does not mock us or sigh in exasperation—He offers His help.

Jesus invites us to come before God's throne of grace. Not slumped in shame or cowering in uncertainty, but courageously—knowing our Father welcomes us. In His presence we will find mercy and power, because Jesus was tempted too.

So step up to the throne of God, lift your needs to Him, seek His aid. Because Jesus was once tempted and He understands.

Father, please show me how to escape this temptation I face.

APRIL 24

OUR CONFIDENCE

The Lord will be your confidence, and will keep your foot from being caught.

PROVERBS 3:26

The barely avoided accident. The surprise check that comes just in time. The sudden catch in our spirit that says all is not as it seems. God often—and in ways we cannot understand—intervenes as the Rescuer in our lives. He watches over those who follow Him, and He helps us avoid the traps of the wicked.

But these moments are only a glimpse into the interventions of God in our lives.

Perhaps one day we'll comprehend completely all the times and ways He has rescued us from destruction. As we learn to trust God more and more fully, our eyes are opened to all the ways His Spirit protects and guides us, showing us how to live and how to share our faith with those around us. Then we can face life not with fear, but with confidence.

Lord, I trust in You to guide and protect me. Because of You, I can walk through this life without fear.

APRIL 25

YOU ARE SAVED

God saved you by his grace when you believed. And you can't take credit for this; it is a gift from God.

EPHESIANS 2:8 NLT

Grace is a gift. We can never earn it, never be worthy of it on our own. Salvation—freedom from all our sins—is also a prize we can never earn. Yet God offers these kindnesses to us freely. He doesn't have to. He isn't forced to. They are what He wants us to have because He loves us so.

As sinners, we deserve the punishment of an eternal separation from our God. But instead, through His grace, we are joined with Christ, made coheirs with Him, and lifted up to the heavens. We no longer have any reason to fear death or judgment. Instead of a cold grave or divine judgment, we have the glories and wonders of heaven to look forward to. All because of God's great gift.

Father, it's through Your grace that I have been saved. Teach me to share Your gift with all the world.

APRIL 26

GOD REMEMBERS

He will not forget how hard you have worked for him.

HEBREWS 6:10 NLT

The life of faith is not a life of idleness. It is busy with serving others, working in God's kingdom, and laboring for His saints. As we serve God, there will be days when we are filled with His joy and a sense of divine purpose and satisfaction. But there will also be other days—days when the people we serve grumble against us or when our labors seem in vain.

It is then that we must remember *why* we serve—not for praise or earthly gain, but to honor our Lord. And though our efforts may seem unimportant or even invisible, God sees all we do and He does not forget. So we must be diligent and not allow ourselves to give up; then we will inherit all the promised blessings of God.

Lord, when I feel as if everything I do is in vain, remind me that You see and honor my efforts.

APRIL 27

WE WILL RISE

Christ is risen from the dead, and has become the firstfruits of those who have fallen asleep.

1 CORINTHIANS 15:20

When Adam sinned, he introduced the concept of death. And not just for Adam, but for all people. When Jesus rose up from death, He became the "firstfruits"—the first of many who will be resurrected from the grave to the eternal life of heaven. Just as death came into the world because of one man, eternal life came into the world because of one Man (vv. 21–22).

Eternal life is offered to all, no matter who we are or what we have done. We have only to believe that Jesus is our Lord, to accept His rule over our lives, and to follow Him. Then, because Christ is risen, one day we too will rise.

Thank You, Lord, for sending Jesus to be the "firstfruits" of the resurrection, so that one day I will rise up too.

APRIL 28

HIS MERCIES ARE NEW

His mercies begin afresh each morning.

LAMENTATIONS 3:23 NLT

When it comes to God, we—thankfully!—do not get what we deserve. Our sins should earn us God's wrath, "for all have sinned and fall short of the glory of God" (Romans 3:23). Yet "we are not consumed"; because we have chosen to live our lives for Him, "His compassions fail not" (Lamentations 3:22).

Even though we are God's own children, we are not perfect. There will be days when our walk with Him is filled with stumblings; when we worry our sins are too many or too great; when we fear we've strayed too often or too far from His path; when we think, *Surely God must have given up on me*. On those days, remember this promise: His mercies "begin afresh" every day.

We cannot exhaust the unmerited compassions, the love, and grace of our God.

Lord, thank You for each morning's fresh supply of mercies.

APRIL 29

FIND YOUR LIFE

"Whoever loses His life for My sake will find it."

MATTHEW 16:25

Take up [your] cross, and follow Me" (v. 24). That's what we must do if we truly want to follow Jesus. But what does it mean? The literal cross of Jesus was fashioned from wood by Roman hands over two thousand years ago. How can we possibly take up His cross?

The cross Jesus speaks of isn't made of wood; it is our lives. We must take all we do and say and think, all we own and love, and surrender them to Jesus. When we give all we are to Jesus—when He is the reason we live and love, the reason we sacrifice our wants and wishes to His will—we have taken up our cross. We may "lose" our own lives, but He leads us to lives beyond anything we could ever imagine.

Lord, I want to find the life You have planned for me. Help me to daily surrender all I am and all I have to You.

APRIL 30

DELIVERED FROM FEARS

I sought the L*ORD*, *and He heard me, and delivered me from all my fears.*

PSALM 34:4

In Psalm 34, David praised God for saving him from his many fears. What fears follow you throughout the day? How much do they affect your daily decisions, your daily joy? Have you tried to free yourself from the anxieties that haunt your soul? Have you experienced, like the psalmist, deliverance from those things? If so, you can understand his praise. To be relieved of fear can feel like finally dropping a burden, lightening an unbearable load.

We praise our God for this miraculous delivery from *all* our fears, including our troubles (v. 6), our wants and needs (v. 9), our heartbreak (v. 18), and our enemies (v. 16).

When we seek God in our prayers, He hears and delivers us from all our fears.

Lord, when I call out to You, You answer. I am so grateful for Your daily deliverance.

MAY

MAY 1

WHAT YOU THINK

As he thinks in his heart, so is he.

PROVERBS 23:7

You are what you think. That's the essence of the message behind Proverbs 23:7. And it's also the impulse behind the words of Philippians 4:8—"Whatever things are true, whatever things are noble, whatever things are just, whatever things are pure, whatever things are lovely . . . meditate on these things." We don't have to ponder long to realize that all those things describe the Lord and His blessings.

If, however, our thoughts focus on those things that are wrong—that are untrue, ignoble, unjust, impure, and ugly—then we will quickly find our hearts and lives headed in that same direction. Our view of the world very much affects how we live in and react to it. When we keep our thoughts fixed firmly on the goodness that comes from above, there is no room for evil thoughts to take root—and our lives will reflect what we think.

Lord, open my eyes to see all Your goodness, so I can live a life that adds Your loveliness to the world.

MAY 2

JESUS IS THE LIGHT

"I am the light of the world. He who follows Me shall not walk in darkness, but have the light of life."

JOHN 8:12

There are two paths we can walk in this world: the path of light or the path of darkness. We choose which to follow. Both paths have obstacles to overcome. Both are difficult and have their struggles. But the path of darkness is . . . dark. Those who follow it stumble along on their own.

The path of light, however, is illuminated by Jesus Himself. Those who follow it have Him to guide them, to help them, to travel beside them each step of the way. To choose this path is to follow Jesus—to confess that He is the Son of God and trust Him as Lord of our lives. When we choose His path, He lights our way—all the way home to heaven.

Jesus, please shine Your light into my life and lead me in the way You want me to go.

MAY 3

THE IMPOSSIBLE IS POSSIBLE

"With men this is impossible, but with God all things are possible."

MATTHEW 19:26

So many times in life we fail to realize that all things are possible through God—He is the God of infinite possibilities. When Jesus spoke these words in Matthew 19:26, He was talking about the ability to choose serving God's kingdom over earthly riches. But any time we strive to choose God's will over our own selfish wills, God steps in to make what the world would declare impossible possible.

Psalm 37:4 says, "Delight yourself also in the LORD, and He shall give you the desires of your heart." It's not that we get everything we want, but that we learn to want everything God wants. When we choose to spend time with God, to honor Him, live for Him, and serve Him with all our hearts, we can find true contentment in all the possibilities of our God.

Lord, when I think I can't do what You ask of me, remind me that You make the impossible possible.

MAY 4

THE SHELTER OF HIS WINGS

Show Your marvelous lovingkindness . . . save those who trust in You from those who rise up against them. Keep me as the apple of Your eye; hide me under the shadow of Your wings.

PSALM 17:7–8

Like a mother hen protecting her chicks, the Lord spreads open the shelter of His wings and invites us to hide under their shadow. What a beautiful and comforting image! When enemies surround and attack, the Lord is our refuge. As we seek our sanctuary in Him, He shows the depth of His "marvelous lovingkindness": He protects us from those who rise up against us, He cherishes us as the apple of His eye, and He shelters us under His wings.

When the days are dark and our enemies are strong, we must remember who has the power to save us—He is our Rock, our Fortress, our Deliverer (Psalm 18:2). He is faithful to save those who trust in Him, tucking us safely under His wings.

Lord, Your lovingkindness toward me is endless—and for that I praise You always.

MAY 5

GOD IS ALWAYS NEAR

As the mountains surround Jerusalem, so the L*ORD* *surrounds His people from this time forth and forever.*

PSALM 125:2

God's Word frequently reminds us of His continual presence (Matthew 28:20; Deuteronomy 31:6; Hebrews 13:5). As we walk with God and keep Him the Lord and Master of our lives, let's remember that He has promised to be with us always. We can take advantage of the fact that we can have constant communication with Him as we live each day in His presence. Can you comprehend what a gift this is?

Make it your prayer to be keenly aware of His sweet presence that guides, comforts, and strengthens. Delight in Him who chooses to stay near His people—near you—at all times.

Father, You have promised to stay close to me. Remind me of this promise when I feel alone or afraid.

MAY 6

GOD DELIGHTS IN YOU

He also brought me out into a broad place; He delivered me because He delighted in me.

PSALM 18:19

You may be blessed to have someone who seems to love everything about you, who enjoys simply being with you. What a source of joy! But did you know that the Almighty God, your Creator, delights in you as well? Look at the evidence:

- He loves you so much He sent His Son to save you (John 3:16).
- His love is so lavish that He calls you His own child (1 John 3:1).
- He even rejoices over you with song (Zephaniah 3:17).

The longer and the more closely you walk with Him, the greater will be your delight in Him . . . and the greater His delight in you!

Lord, the magnitude of Your love astonishes me. Let me never stop delighting in You.

MAY 7

GOD IS FOR US

If God is for us, who can ever be against us?

ROMANS 8:31 NLT

God is on our side! That may sound overly simplistic, but we need to cling to that basic truth when the world undermines and even attacks our faith in Jesus. Our culture is becoming increasingly hostile to believers. It is a very real battle, but God has promised to guard our hearts and minds.

We also need to remember that God is on our side when we consider the fact that Satan is a stronger, deadlier enemy than any of the world's threats or weapons. Eternity is at stake in the battle that matters most—the battle between holiness and evil, the battle for our souls. But God promises to protect His people and in truth, He has already won (John 12:31).

Lord, even though some days it is hard to be a believer, I will never stop trusting in You.

MAY 8

EVERLASTING BEAUTY

The things which are seen are temporary, but the things which are not seen are eternal.

2 CORINTHIANS 4:18

When we think of beauty, we tend to look in the mirror and "reflect" on what we see. But eventually the outward beauty we possess will change and fade away. There is, however, a beauty that does not fade away. This beauty shines out from within us as we allow the love of God to rule our lives. In turn God will work within us to change our priorities and to make us more and more like Him.

If we love the Lord, we will make it our aim and our delight to please Him by the way we live. We should look for ways to make Him smile. Let your light so shine that others will see the gift of His love, a beauty that is eternal.

Father God, focus my eyes and my thoughts on the things of eternal beauty, not outward beauty.

MAY 9

CHRIST LIVES IN US

I have been crucified with Christ; it is no longer I who live, but Christ lives in me.

GALATIANS 2:20

The apostle Paul said, "I have been crucified with Christ." When we choose to follow Jesus—to live as He wants us to live—we die to the persons we were. We die to our self-centeredness and devotion to self-satisfaction. To be crucified with Christ means we are redeemed before God. We can lay aside trying to work our way to heaven. We are free from the burden of nitpicky law-keeping. We can instead enjoy life in the freedom of Christ's salvation. Not a freedom to continue sinning, but a freedom to come before God, washed clean of our sins (Romans 6:1–4).

We no longer live in the selfishness of our flesh; we live in the selflessness of Christ. We yield ourselves to the will of Christ. And when we do that, Christ comes to live in and through us.

Lord, I surrender every word, thought, and action to You. Live in Me so others see only You.

MAY 10

OUR GUIDE FOR LIFE

I will pursue your commands, for you expand my understanding.

PSALM 119:32 NLT

God cares about each of us so much that He has given us a guide for life. That guide is the Bible, and all of us are to be students of that Book throughout our lives. We grow in our faith, we are enabled to share our beliefs more clearly, and we gain a big-picture perspective on the course of history when we regularly spend time learning what God wants us to know about His love and His ways.

God desires that His children know all we can about Him and how to live in a way that honors Him. The psalmist declared he would seek out God's commands in order to "expand [his] understanding." This knowledge and wisdom are available to us in the Bible. It is our guide for this life, and our guide to eternal life.

Father, thank You for the gift of Your Word.
Teach me to be guided by its wisdom.

MAY 11

DON'T GIVE UP

We [endure] by keeping our eyes on Jesus . . .
who initiates and perfects our faith.

HEBREWS 12:2 NLT

We've all experienced times when circumstances are overwhelming, people are difficult, and relationships seem hopeless. Beaten down and exhausted, you just want to throw up your hands in defeat.

When you find yourself in a place like that, remember that you are not alone. Despite what your feelings may suggest, God, the One for whom nothing is impossible, is with you and goes before you. You may feel discouraged, but God will give you the wisdom you need to carry on through the next moment, the next hour, the next day. The Bible describes Jesus as the One who "initiates and perfects our faith"; therefore let's look to Him when we need endurance. He will help us not only to bear up through this present situation, but to be a light for Him in it.

Lord, strengthen me to get through this situation
and help me to be gracious as I do.

MAY 12

RENEWED YOUTH

Bless the Lord, O my soul . . . who satisfies your mouth with good things, so that your youth is renewed like the eagle's.

PSALM 103:2, 5

No matter how old you are now, aging can be jarring. After all, you probably still feel as if you're eighteen or thirty-five on the inside. But give thanks to God that these years are part of His good plan for you. Choose to celebrate the ways He has shaped your life for your good and His glory. And acknowledge that He has promised you will "bear fruit in old age" (Psalm 92:14).

If today you're feeling your age (or even older), ask Him to show you where and how to bear that fruit. He will. Perhaps it's sharing your life with someone younger; being a mentor will mean blessings for you and blessings for those you come alongside. And what happens when you realize the Lord is using you in another's life? You're energized and "your youth is renewed like the eagle's"!

Lord, make me a blessing in someone else's life, and please bless me with renewed strength.

MAY 13

A PERFECT WAY

Who is a rock, except our God? It is God who arms me with strength, and makes my way perfect.

PSALM 18:31–32

God's way is perfect, and when we follow Him, He makes our way perfect. Perhaps not perfect by this world's definition, but perfect by His as He teaches us to trust in Him and to be more like Him each day.

He is our Shield, protecting us from our enemies. He is our Rock, the solid foundation we can build our life upon—so that, like the wise man, we can not only survive but stand strong when the storms come (Matthew 7:24–25). And when we begin to feel weak, He arms us with His strength, which has no limits and no end.

As we faithfully and trustingly follow Him, the Lord blesses us and makes our way perfect—leading us ever closer to Him.

Lord, I place my life in Your hands. I trust You to make my way perfect.

MAY 14

PROMISES FOR ALL

There is neither Jew nor Greek, there is neither slave nor free, there is neither male nor female; for you are all one in Christ Jesus.

GALATIANS 3:28

God's promises are available to everyone and anyone. The salvation of Christ is freely offered to every single person on earth. God does not discriminate. He does not look at outward appearances as man does; He looks at the heart (1 Samuel 16:7). He does not care about race or gender or socioeconomic standings. God cares about people. Period.

Anyone can claim the love of God. Anyone can have sins forgiven and shortcomings forgotten. And anyone can become brand-new in Christ—"a new creation" (2 Corinthians 5:17). All of us can live with joy in our hearts as the children of a loving and caring heavenly Father . . . if we choose to do so.

Lord, You offer Your salvation to anyone who comes to You. Help me to be as accepting and loving as You.

MAY 15

THE ABSOLUTE AUTHORITY

Forever, O Lord, Your word is settled in heaven.

PSALM 119:89

Simply put, if it's in the Bible, we can believe it's true. The words in Scripture were given by the inspiration of God (2 Timothy 3:16) and are completely authoritative for every Christian. They are also the light that illumines our way and a road map for living lives that honor Jesus. God's Word gives us the instructions we need to live each day in obedience to Him.

But God's Word is much more than a set of instructions, a map, or a book of law. It is letter of love written to His children. It is our source of encouragement and hope, courage and strength. It is wisdom and the way to the perfect peace and joy of God. It is the voice of God breathed out onto paper pages and the absolute authority for our lives.

Lord, thank You for Your Word, for its hope and encouragement and strength. Guide me in its wisdom.

MAY 16

THOSE WHO BLESS

"Inasmuch as you did it to one of the least of these My brethren, you did it to Me."

MATTHEW 25:40

You've probably noticed that actions often speak much louder than words. So think for a minute about what your actions say about you: Do they suggest that you are living for yourself, or do people see something different about the way you speak, work, and interact with others? Do your actions and words shine with God's love and the joy of being in His presence, no matter how tough life's circumstances become?

The way you walk and talk are opportunities to let God love others through you. Do you reach out to the poor and hurting? Do you help the sick? Do you treat the homeless lady with the same respect as the lady who sits next to you at church? For whatever you do for the "least of these," you've done for Jesus. Make sure Your actions are ones He will bless.

Lord, help me treat "the least of these" the way You treat them.

MAY 17

HE CARES FOR US

Humble yourselves under the mighty hand of God, that He may exalt you in due time, casting all your care upon Him, for He cares for you.

1 PETER 5:6–7

When God invites us to let Him carry our cares, He is not merely offering a listening ear; He is offering to shoulder the load we bear. He sees our burdens and wants to help us with them. Why? Because "He cares."

But to cast our cares upon someone else, even God, is a humbling thing. It means admitting we can't take care of our troubles ourselves. That's not a very popular idea in our self-reliant world. But when we do choose to humble ourselves and submit our lives to the mighty guiding hand of God, He promises that one day He will lift us up—all the way up to a heavenly home with Him. So let us cast our concerns upon Him, knowing we can trust Him to care for us.

Lord, I give my worries, my whole life, to You.
Thank You for inviting me to do so.

MAY 18

LIFE-GIVING POWER

The LORD is my strength and my shield; my heart trusted in Him, and I am helped.

PSALM 28:7

Sometimes life is difficult. We face many challenges and disappointments that are hard to accept. But we have a heavenly Father who cares deeply for us in every way. And thankfully, He goes beyond caring to providing.

God has given us His Word to guide and provide us the wisdom to withstand any situation that life brings. We have only to open the Book of Life to find comfort and hope. Our heavenly Father also gives us His strength when we are tired and life-giving power when we are weak. He is our Rock to stand on and our Shield to protect us. And when we turn to our God in complete trust, He is faithful to help.

Lord, You are my Strength and Shield. Thank You for caring, protecting, and providing.

MAY 19

GOD ALWAYS WINS

We know that all things work together for good to those who love God, to those who are the called according to His purpose.

ROMANS 8:28

On this side of heaven, we will never understand how "all things" can possibly work together for good for God's children. Some things, yes. But all things? That's more difficult.

Of course we recognize that not all things are themselves inherently good, but we trust our God and believe that He truly desires what is best for us. He is able to bring joy out of sadness, triumph out of tragedy.

When facing tough times, lean on the Lord for strength, courage, and the will to handle the challenges of life. Keep in mind that "if God is for us, who can be against us?" (Romans 8:31). Nothing can ultimately triumph over us, for in the end, God always wins, and we win with Him.

Lord, I believe You are able to bring some good out of all things—help me see that goodness.

MAY 20

WE WILL ABIDE

Let that abide in you which you heard from the beginning.
If what you heard from the beginning abides in you,
you also will abide in the Son and in the Father.

1 JOHN 2:24

These verses from 1 John were a warning to new believers about false teachers. And it's a warning that we do well to heed, especially in these days. Technology makes it possible for information to spread like wildfire—regardless of whether the information is true. This is particularly dangerous when it comes to false teachings about God.

Fortunately God does not leave us to puzzle out which people and ideas are from Him. We have the Holy Bible to show us the way. Through unchanging principles, examples, and true-life accounts we can see how others sifted the true from the false. When we ensure that God's truth abides in us, we will abide in God.

Lord, remind me to test everything I hear about You against the perfect truth of Your Word.

MAY 21

OUR COMPLETE SALVATION

Christ was offered once to bear the sins of many. To those who eagerly wait for Him He will appear a second time, apart from sin, for salvation.

HEBREWS 9:28

When Jesus came to earth as a man, He gave His life "that whoever believes in Him should not perish but have everlasting life" (John 3:16). With His death on the cross, He defeated the power of sin to condemn us. That was the first step toward our salvation.

As believers we "eagerly" await Jesus' return. We know that when He comes again, He will gather His people to live with Him in the kingdom of heaven. Sin, failure, and anguish will be forgotten as we embrace resurrection life. Because Jesus bore "the sins of many," as believers we will never bear those sins ourselves. So we watch for His coming, for His promised return.

Father, thank You for Jesus, for the price He paid on the cross, and for the promised day I will join You in heaven.

MAY 22

JESUS WILL COME IN

"Behold, I stand at the door and knock. If anyone hears My voice and opens the door, I will come in to him and dine with him, and he with Me."

REVELATION 3:20–22

As the saying goes, we are the kings of our own castles. Similarly, we are the kings of our own hearts. We decide who comes and goes, who receives our loyalty and love. It is we who must open the door to allow anyone inside. Even Jesus asks permission to enter. Though He will stand outside and knock all the days of our lives, He will never force His way in.

But if we open the door and ask Jesus in, He gives us this wondrous promise: "I will come in to him and dine with him, and he with Me."

What is the state of your heart? Is it barred to Jesus? Or is it unlocked and standing open, ready for Jesus to step inside?

Lord Jesus, come into my life. Dine with me, live with me, be in me always.

MAY 23

FAITHFULNESS IS REWARDED

I have fought the good fight, I have finished the race, I have kept the faith. Finally, there is laid up for me the crown of righteousness.

2 TIMOTHY 4:7–8

Paul's life in the service of Jesus and the gospel was not an easy one. Opposition, enemies, prison, beatings, shipwreck: Paul continuously confronted difficulty. Yet with the strength and power of the Lord, he "fought the good fight" and "finished the race." For that he would receive the reward of a crown of righteousness. But that crown isn't just for Paul, it is for all of us!

Like Paul, and with God's guidance, we can devote our lives to following the course the Lord has laid out for us. With His courage, we can fight the good fight. With His strength, we can finish the race. And because we keep the faith, keep following Christ, there is waiting for us the crown of righteousness. One day the Lord Himself will present it to us.

Lord, guide and strengthen me to finish this race faithfully so that I might one day wear the crown of righteousness.

MAY 24

HE HELPS US FORGIVE

God is working in you, giving you the desire and the power to do what pleases him.

PHILIPPIANS 2:13 NLT

Every single one of God's commands is good for us, and He clearly commands us to forgive others (Matthew 6:14). If obeying God isn't reason enough to forgive, realize that when you harbor anger and resentment toward someone, you are hardening your heart. Too much of that can make your heart impenetrable, even by God's love. God warns us against this act (Hebrews 3:8).

A wise person once observed, "Not forgiving is like drinking poison and waiting for the other person to die." So yes, acknowledge your feelings, but at the same time look beyond your circumstances to your holy and forgiving God. He can and will give you "the desire and the power to do what pleases him."

Lord, in spite of all my struggles and troubles, You've given me Your mercy. Help me to be merciful too.

MAY 25

ALL WE NEED

God is able to bless you abundantly, so that in all things at all times, having all that you need, you will abound in every good work.

2 CORINTHIANS 9:8 NIV

God will bless us with what we need—and that includes *being* what we need—in order for us to do His good will. This is a promise the Lord gives us. Whatever we need God to be, He is. But notice that He doesn't promise to be whatever we want. He will never be a God who gives us permission to sin if we feel like it, or if everyone else is doing it. He will never give us what we need to abound in sin. But He will give us what we need to do His will.

God gives strength to the weak, shade to those fainting in the scorching sun, comfort when life seems unfair, and joy when we walk closely with Him. He wipes away our tears, holds us close, and shows us the way to go. *He* is what we need.

Lord, thank You for being all and everything I need. I find my joy in following You.

MAY 26

HIS SONS AND DAUGHTERS

"I will dwell in them and walk among them. I will be their God, and they shall be My people. . . . I will be a Father to you, and you shall be My sons and daughters."

2 CORINTHIANS 6:16, 18

Read again this beautiful promise of God: "I will dwell in them and walk among them." We need never worry about the presence of God. We can turn to Him at any time, as often as we need, for strength, wisdom, and reassurance. He will equip us to do what we could never do on our own.

The loving care God demonstrates toward us is unending—and so should be our praises to Him. His promises are rich and numerous, and they are designed to lead us closer to Him. But those promises do not just fall into our laps. We have to claim them and their power by first choosing God as the Lord of our lives. Then He shall call us "My sons and daughters" and dwell with us always.

Lord, that You would call me Your own child is amazing. Thank You for a love so great!

MAY 27

WHEREVER WE GO

If I ride the wings of the morning, if I dwell by the farthest oceans, even there your hand will guide me, and your strength will support me.

PSALM 139:9–10 NLT

Psalm 139 spells out for us a simple truth: God is everywhere. No place exists where God is not. Where can we flee from His Spirit, His presence? Not the heights of heaven or the depths of hell. Not the "uttermost parts of the sea" (v. 9), or anywhere in between. Wherever we go, He is there.

But God can also be found in all the less-literal places. He is in the midst of that messy marriage, disastrous job, dysfunctional family, and sinful situation. Though we may ignore or even deny His presence, He is there. So claim this promise: there is nowhere you can go that God is not. *Everywhere* His hand is waiting to hold you.

Lord, Your presence in my life is everything to me. Guide me and lead me, hold me by the hand.

MAY 28

ALL THINGS NEW

He who sat on the throne said, "Behold, I make all things new."

REVELATION 21:5

Society is filled with programs, articles, and advertisements telling us how to stay young, lose weight, and be more desirable. Our eternal optimism keeps us striving to achieve those things. Thankfully, God offers us a better hope.

With God, we will grow older . . . and better. Walking by His side, over time, we learn to experience a richness of life and steadiness of faith that renews, strengthens, and encourages us. Despite all the emphasis modern culture places on youth, a person whose self-esteem and self-identity are rooted in a relationship with God is a person who can age with dignity and grace. If we invite God's Spirit to live in us, then our spirits will be made brand-new every day. "Behold," says the Lord, "I make all things new." And He does.

Lord, the days go by so quickly. Teach me to slow down and enjoy each moment with You.

MAY 29

GOD IS DEPENDABLE

Blessed be the Lord*. . . . There has not failed one word of all His good promise, which He promised through His servant Moses.*

1 KINGS 8:56

Your car won't start. Your job suddenly disappears. Your friend forgot your birthday. The people and things of the world are sometimes reliable . . . and sometimes not. But God is completely, irrevocably trustworthy. Not one word of His promises will ever fail.

Just consider some of the examples of the faithfulness of our unchanging God. He said He would lead Abraham, and He did. God said He would make a way through the Red Sea, and He did. God said He would send His Son to take away our sins, and He did. So when God says He will lead, He will make a way, He will save us . . . we know every word of His promises will come to fruition. Unlike the things and people of this world, He is absolutely dependable.

Lord, it's hard to know whom I can count on, but I know that You will never let me down.

MAY 30

LIGHT IN THE GRAY

The eyes of the LORD are on the righteous,
and His ears are open to their cry.

PSALM 34:15

Sometimes the world seems gray. *Dark* gray. Sometimes you know why, but other times you don't. Whatever its source, that grayness can weigh you down and steal your energy and enthusiasm for life. It can cause you to isolate yourself, and it can make doubts grow to daunting proportions. But the truth in God's Word can shine light into the gray.

Choose to believe God's promise that even if you don't feel hope and even if you can't imagine how good could happen, He will bring beauty out of the ashes. He will exchange joy for mourning and a garment of praise for this gray heaviness (Isaiah 61:3). Your almighty Savior does all that because He dearly loves you. And because you are His and because He is God, no one can take away His love for you.

Lord, when no sunlight penetrates the haze, send Your light to chase away the grayness.

MAY 31

ALL THE ANSWERS WE NEED

Through Your precepts I get understanding. . . . Your word is a lamp to my feet and a light to my path.

PSALM 119:104–105

In today's noisy world with its many voices calling us in different directions, it's easy to find ourselves confused. The loud and contradictory messages the world speaks about what to believe and how to live can cause uncertainty about who we are as people or even as children of God.

By God's grace, though, He has provided His Word of truth. Unlike our noisy world, it doesn't change with the fashions or trending opinions. We can open the pages of Scripture and find all the answers we need.

When the world gets too noisy, step away and spend quiet time alone with Him by reading and believing His promises to you. He will direct your path toward peace, contentment, and clarity—gifts only He can give.

Lord, please guide me as I try to live a life that pleases You in this confusing world.

JUNE

JUNE 1

GOD'S OWN TREASURE

"Are not two sparrows sold for a copper coin? And not one of them falls to the ground apart from your Father's will. . . . Do not fear therefore; you are of more value than many sparrows."

MATTHEW 10:29–31

In Jesus' day, two sparrows were sold for the price of a single coin. Though they held no value in the world's eyes, each one was known by the Father and included in His will. If each sparrow is so precious to Him, how much more precious are we—the creation who seeks to know and please Him?

We are God's own treasure, and He wants us to understand that He cares for us with not only an everlasting love, but a deeply personal love. When we surrender our lives to His will and follow Him faithfully, we have no need to dread anything. Our Lord, who knows each sparrow, promises that we are worth much more than they—and He will keep watch over us (Psalm 121:3).

Lord, thank You for knowing me personally and loving me so much. I will trust in You and not be afraid.

JUNE 2

IF WE BELIEVE, WE RECEIVE

"Whoever says to this mountain, 'Be removed and be cast into the sea,' and does not doubt in his heart, but believes that those things he says will be done, he will have whatever he says."

MARK 11:23

Faith moves mountains. When we pray—not in doubt, but in trusting belief that God will do His will—the larger-than-life problems in our lives move. Sometimes with a miraculous, all-at-once casting into the sea, and sometimes stone by stone.

Sometimes we're certain about what God wants in a given situation. In those cases it's easy to pray boldly. But even if we wonder what God's will is, we can pray believing He will answer with what is best for us.

When you live in the Lord's presence, you can be assured of answered prayer before the answer actually comes—and "whatever things you ask when you pray, believe that you receive them, and you will have them" (v. 24).

Lord, shape my prayers to reflect Your will;
I will trust You with my mountains.

JUNE 3

GRACE FOR YOU

All have sinned and fall short of the glory of God, being justified freely by His grace through the redemption that is in Christ Jesus.

ROMANS 3:23–24

Have you ever wondered, *Does God really love me, a sinner who's wandered so far from Him?* God answers that question over and over again in His Word, but perhaps one of the greatest testimonials of His love is found in John 3:17: "God did not send His Son into the world to condemn the world, but that the world through Him might be saved." God didn't wait until we were perfect to send His Son; He didn't wait until we were worthy.

God's love is based on His grace. There's nothing we must do to win His love. He loves us because of who we are—His creation (Genesis 1:27). He offers His grace to us because of who He is—love (1 John 4:8). You are loved, and His grace is for you.

Thank You, Lord, for Your unconditional love and Your unmerited grace.

JUNE 4

GOD WILL HELP

I will call upon God, and the LORD shall save me. Evening and morning and at noon I will pray, and cry aloud, and He shall hear my voice.

PSALM 55:16–17

On this side of heaven, we may never understand why God allows us to experience certain tough times, unexpected hurts, or devastating setbacks. Trying to figure out God and His reasons is futile. His ways are not like our ways (Isaiah 55:8). But we can be sure that He is all-powerful, all-loving, all-wise, and all-good.

Whether we are in a season of calm or crisis, God is with us. So when we do face a crisis, we must go to Him in prayer and ask Him to lead us, guide us, even carry us. Our almighty God has promised to answer us whenever we call upon Him; He has promised to be with us in times of trouble. We can rely on His promises. On every single one.

Lord, I lift up my troubles to You, trusting You to take care of me. Please show me the right thing to do and say.

JUNE 5

WE WILL BE RAISED

"This is the will of Him who sent Me, that everyone who sees the Son and believes in Him may have everlasting life; and I will raise him up at the last day."

JOHN 6:40

We were created to do God's will—to love Him, to serve Him, to follow Him all the days of our lives. He is the Father, and we are His children. So obedience is just a natural part of our relationship. Even Jesus, when He explained why He stepped down from heaven, declared that it was not to do whatever He wanted; it was to do His Father's will (v. 38).

Jesus—the Son of God—became an obedient servant to fulfill the will of the One who sent Him. And what was His Father's will? "That everyone who sees the Son and believes in Him may have everlasting life"—an everlasting life made possible because Jesus came and removed the one obstacle that kept us separated from God: our sins. When we believe, we want to obey as Jesus did. And when we believe, we will be raised.

Lord, lead me to obey You in all things, just as Jesus did.

JUNE 6

FAITH WILL ABOUND

As you therefore have received Christ Jesus the Lord, so walk in Him, rooted and built up in Him and established in the faith, as you have been taught, abounding in it with thanksgiving.

COLOSSIANS 2:6–7

How do you define *faith*? The Bible tells us, "Faith is confidence in what we hope for and assurance about what we do not see" (Hebrews 11:1 NIV). It is believing God will do what He promises to do, then acting on that belief.

As we go through our lives encountering joys and obstacles, facing enemies and making friends, handling extraordinary joys and losses, we live by faith in Him who saves us. We keep going, putting one foot in front of the other, trusting that He really will guide, teach, protect, and provide for us, that He will take us home to heaven with Him one day. That is what it means to live by faith. And when we do, our faith is not only "established," it abounds.

Lord, I know You will keep Your promises. I put my faith in You.

JUNE 7

OUR LABORS COUNT

Be steadfast, immovable, always abounding in the work of the Lord, knowing that your labor is not in vain in the Lord.

1 CORINTHIANS 15:58

Through God's grace and Jesus' sacrifice, sin and the grave have been defeated. Out of gratitude for these great and eternal gifts, we labor for our Lord. We serve Him with sacrifices of our time, our talents, our money.

But our efforts aren't always appreciated, humanly speaking. Sometimes they are simply unnoticed; other times they are scorned. We might even start to wonder why we bother. When doubts plague you, remember this: "Nothing you do for the Lord is ever useless" (NLT).

Our work for God has value and meaning because God gives us the gifts and strength to accomplish it. He sees all, and He will honor us for every act we do in His service. Our "labor is not in vain in the Lord."

Lord, lead me to serve You faithfully, knowing that everything I do for You counts for Your glory.

JUNE 8

KEEP PRAYING

Pray without ceasing.

1 THESSALONIANS 5:17

Do you think it's possible to pray unceasingly? Was Paul tasking us with something we honestly cannot carry out?

Let's consider our definition of prayer. It is not always a kneeling-down, eyes-closed communication with God—though that is essential at times. Prayer is also an attitude of continually turning toward God. It is looking for His presence in every moment. It is making Him the center of our lives so that seeking Him becomes our first response in every situation, whether joyful or painful. We practice ceaseless prayer when our thoughts fill with Him as naturally as our lungs fill with air.

If God wants us to pray without ceasing, He wants us to come to Him with everything, no matter how small. Pray knowing God wants to hear from you.

Father, turn my thoughts always to You, so that I may learn to pray without ceasing.

JUNE 9

RISE ABOVE

This is the love of God, that we keep His commandments. And His commandments are not burdensome.

1 JOHN 5:3

Our society doesn't care much for obedience. It views rules as shackles that keep people from doing what they want to do. But the Lord's commandments "are not burdensome." They are God's way to say, "I love you." They protect us and guide us toward what is best for us. They actually help us both avoid the pitfalls of sin and overcome the obstacles of living in a fallen world. Because of faith—and the obedience that stems from that faith—God lifts us up above the muck and mire of this world, sets us high upon a rock (Psalm 40:2), and enables us to overcome (1 John 5:4).

Can you begin to see obedience as a means of loving the Lord? How will that affect your daily outlook?

Father, help me show You my love by always seeking to honor and obey You.

JUNE 10

OTHERS WILL HELP

Let us consider one another in order to stir up love and good works . . . exhorting one another.

HEBREWS 10:24–25

You are important to other Christians—to their faith and their growth in Christlikeness—and they are important to you.

You gain strength and find encouragement when you spend time with your fellow Christians. Sharing your struggles will result in blessings of care, compassion, and prayer. You, in turn, can supply the same blessings when others are struggling.

In His Word, God cautions you not to neglect spending time with fellow believers (v. 25). This is important especially when you are hurting. In fact, God will send other believers to help you, providing comfort, guidance, or a shoulder to lean upon. Whether you're on the giving or the receiving end, He will bless you through the members of His family.

Lord, thank You for those You put in my life who point me to You. Help me to be that same light for others.

JUNE 11

WE ARE LOVED

This is real love—not that we loved God, but that he loved us and sent his Son as a sacrifice to take away our sins.

1 JOHN 4:10 NLT

Scripture tells us that God loved us from the beginning, even *before* the beginning. And God knew, before we were ever created, that we would need a Savior. So before we came to be, God planned to send His Son to save us: "[Christ] indeed was foreordained before the foundation of the world" (1 Peter 1:20).

So when the time was right, Jesus came and paid the price for the forgiveness of our sins (Galatians 4:4–5). He came to fulfill a promise God made, remembered, and kept. That is how much God loves us. Because of that great love, we are then called to offer the gift of love to those around us. For He who loved us first calls us to love others in the same way (1 John 4:11).

Lord, You have shared Your love so lavishly with me. Help me to be generous with mine.

JUNE 12

WE CAN WORSHIP

"The hour is coming, and now is, when the true worshipers will worship the Father in spirit and truth."

JOHN 4:23

For so many years, those who sought to worship God had to make blood sacrifices and perform ritual cleansings. Priests spoke to God on behalf of the people. In so many ways, the people were separated from the actual presence of God.

But no more. Jesus came, and the curtain between us and God was torn in two (Matthew 27:51). God no longer requires rituals, sacrifices, or priests. Instead He seeks hearts willing to worship Him "in spirit and truth." In spirit, as His Holy Spirit works in our spirits so we come before God in real worship. And in the truth that Jesus is the Son of God, our Savior, who made it possible for each of us to personally worship our God.

Lord, thank You for the privilege of worshiping You in Your presence.

JUNE 13

FINISH THE RACE

Let us strip off every weight that slows us down, especially the sin that so easily trips us up. And let us run with endurance.

HEBREWS 12:1 NLT

The Christian life is like a marathon. To complete it we'll need self-control and perseverance. And we'll also need to run "light," without anything weighing us down. Are you carrying anything that is harming rather than helping you in your race? Perhaps it's burdens from the past, unhealthy relationships, or guilt from long-ago sins. Or perhaps it's the love of money, power, or stuff. What is the sin that "trips [you] up"?

As you release those weights to Jesus, your step will grow lighter and the race will seem more manageable. Take it one mile at a time. As you run, ever seeking Jesus and His Way, He promises to be right there with you, helping you finish the race.

Lord, let me run the race trusting Jesus to help me finish.

JUNE 14

THE SPIRIT WILL GUIDE

"When He, the Spirit of truth, has come, He will guide you into all truth; for He will not speak on His own authority, but whatever He hears He will speak."

JOHN 16:13

Jesus promised that the Holy Spirit would come and guide His people. Note that Jesus didn't promise that the Holy Spirit would take over and live our lives for us. The Holy Spirit never controls people's choices. Instead He directs us, points us in the right direction. The choice to heed His voice and obey—or not—is always ours and ours alone.

We can trust the Spirit to guide us because He doesn't speak from His own authority; He speaks only what He hears from God. Therefore His guidance will be flawless, loving, wise, and faithful to the Word of God. What a gift from the Lord—an indwelling Spirit who leads us in the right way to live and to love and serve our God.

Father, I choose to let Your Spirit guide my every thought and action.

JUNE 15

MARVELOUS WORKS

Seek the Lord and His strength; seek His face evermore! Remember His marvelous works which He has done.

1 CHRONICLES 16:11–12

When you choose to live with Jesus as your Savior and Lord, you will know blessings beyond your imagining. There are the blessings of being in relationship with the holy and almighty God of all creation—the unconditional love, the unending grace and mercy, His abiding presence. Then there is the blessing of being able to serve Him, which yields an abundance of joy and sense of purpose.

Followers of Jesus are also blessed by the gift of Jesus' Holy Spirit, the Comforter, the Teacher, the Guide, who is always with us. The world offers many distractions, loud voices, fleeting pleasures, and heartbreaking pain, but the Spirit will help us keep our eyes on the Lord so we can experience the richness of walking through life with Him—and bear witness to all the marvelous works He does.

Lord, teach me to see Your amazing works and to praise You for each and every one.

JUNE 16

STRENGTH FOR EACH DAY

As your days, so shall your strength be.

DEUTERONOMY 33:25

Consider this: if you are struggling, God wants to use this time to strengthen your faith. The more you persevere and stand against temptation, the more you strengthen your faith muscle. And as you've surely already discovered, life gives you plenty of opportunities to work out this muscle. But when troubles come, do not fear. God promises to supply the strength you need, day by day.

As you surrender control over your life, obey Him, and see His response to that obedience, you will become a stronger and more mature believer. So develop the habit of running to the Lord whenever you face difficult decisions or challenging circumstances. He will hear your requests, show you the way to go, and give you the ability to do His will—supplying the power you need as you live each day by faith.

Lord, in this time of struggle, please show me Your way, supply Your strength, and grow my faith.

JUNE 17

A HOLY LIFE

He himself is fair and just, and he makes sinners right in his sight when they believe in Jesus.

ROMANS 3:26 NLT

Perhaps you feel pain today because of a struggle with sin. If so, then the apostle Paul's words could be yours: "I want to do what is right, but I can't. I want to do what is good, but I don't" (Romans 7:18–19 NLT). When you struggle with sin, know that Jesus, by his victory over sin on the cross, offers you forgiveness (1 John 1:9) and God declares you "right in his sight."

The Spirit is at work within you, transforming you to make you more like Jesus, so don't lose hope about changing sinful habits. Forgiven for your sins, made righteous by God Himself, and empowered by the Holy Spirit, you can freely and boldly live a holy life that points others to Jesus.

Lord, when I stumble in my obedience, please remind me of Your forgiveness and transforming power.

JUNE 18

A CLEAN SLATE

Behold! The Lamb of God who takes away the sin of the world!

JOHN 1:29

The forgiveness of sin is one of God's greatest gifts to those who are in Christ. The slate has been wiped clean, and God has promised never to remember or mention our sins again. Because of God's total, unconditional, and abundant love, He chooses not only to forgive our sins but also to remove them from His presence forever.

The beauty of God's forgiveness opens the door for each of us to have the relationship with Him that He wants and we need. His love overshadows every sin we have committed. God's mercy does not give us the freedom to sin, expecting more forgiveness; rather it gives us the freedom to move past the mistakes we have made and into a deeper, richer relationship with Him and with those we love.

Lord, thank You for wiping my slate clean so I may have an eternal relationship with You.

JUNE 19

HUNGRY FOR BREAD

"I am the bread of life. He who comes to Me shall never hunger, and he who believes in Me shall never thirst."

JOHN 6:35

Sixteen hundred years ago Saint Augustine commented on the fact that within every human heart is a "God-shaped hole." That hole exists because nothing and no one except Jesus will satisfy your desire for love, your quest for purpose, your hope for fulfillment. In short, nothing will feed your heart's hunger except the Bread of Life Himself.

When you realize this truth—when you consider that a God-shaped hole in your heart may be contributing to whatever frustration or dissatisfaction you're dealing with today—life becomes simpler. Your focus is the Lord. When you open your heart and life to Him, He fills you and empowers you to live each moment for Him.

Lord Jesus, come and fill me today. Only You can satisfy my soul's deepest longings.

JUNE 20

BLESSED WITH MERCY

"Blessed are the merciful, for they shall obtain mercy."

MATTHEW 5:7

Mercy is something we all desperately need. Not only from God, but also from others. We all stumble. We all trip over our own tongues and selfish desires.

Thankfully, we serve a merciful God. And as His children, we have the blessing of waking up each morning to a new day, full of fresh mercies (Lamentations 3:22–23). God's mercy is promised to us.

But in order to receive God's promised mercy, we also have a responsibility: to offer that same mercy to others. It's so easy—and often tempting—to dismiss people as hopeless, especially if they've hurt us. But God asks us to do something else instead: to love, to pray for, to forgive, to offer new mercies. Because that's what He does for us.

Lord, help me set aside my own feelings of frustration with others and offer mercy, kindness, and love instead.

JUNE 21

ALL BEAUTIFUL FLOWERS

"Look at the lilies of the field. . . . If God cares so wonderfully for wildflowers that are here today and thrown into the fire tomorrow, he will certainly care for you."

MATTHEW 6:28, 30 NLT

At this gardening time of year, we dive into planting, watering, and weeding. But do you ever wonder who decided which blossoms are flowers and which are weeds? Why is the tiny wild violet a nuisance while the tiny purple phlox is a treasure to be nurtured?

And might we not ask the same question about people? Why are some cast away as unworthy (even from our own Christian circles) while others are cultivated and cared for? While we may make the distinction between flowers and weeds, know that God does not. Christ died to offer salvation to *all* (2 Corinthians 5:15), and here He promises God's care for His cherished children. There are no weeds in His garden, only beautiful, beloved flowers.

Lord, teach me to see every person as worthy of Your love and care.

JUNE 22

GOD'S BEAUTIFUL PLAN

Let us hold fast the confession of our hope without wavering, for He who promised is faithful.

HEBREWS 10:23

God is aware of every situation we encounter, and even though it may sometimes seem impossible, He can fit them all into His master plan for our lives.

We live in a world where problems and difficulties happen daily, where good can turn bad in an instant. But no matter what happens, God promises He will use our experiences—even the hurts, the frustrations, the trials, and the tragedies—for a redeeming purpose. He is Lord of life, during both the good days and the bad moments.

Today, no matter what life throws at you, rest in the promise and the hope that God can weave any situation into His plan for you. And even though you may not yet understand how, He will use it to create a beautiful tapestry of your life.

Lord, You are good, and I trust that Your plans for me are good. Help me keep walking with You.

JUNE 23

NEVER-ENDING LIFE

"Whoever lives and believes in Me shall never die. Do you believe this?"

JOHN 11:26

Jesus spoke the words of this verse to Martha as her brother, Lazarus, lay dead in a tomb. But Jesus wasn't talking only about His ability to raise Lazarus from death; He was also referring to His own coming resurrection and the later resurrection of all believers. And when He spoke of life, He added that those who believe in Him would never die—because His own resurrection would defeat the power of death and gift His believers with eternal life.

Notice Martha's beautiful response in verse 27: "Yes, Lord, I believe." That response of pure faith—a faith that didn't understand but still trusted—is one we should emulate. When we place our faith in Jesus, we can claim His promises of abundant life today and of an eternal, resurrected life when He comes to take us home.

Lord, You *are* the resurrection and the life. I place my life, my heart, my spirit within Your hands.

JUNE 24

GRACE ABOUNDS

We praise God for the glorious grace he has poured out on us who belong to his dear Son.

EPHESIANS 1:6 NLT

God's grace—that bountiful gift from our heavenly Father, purchased by His own Son—does more than erase sin. God's grace can also bring peace, hope, and healing. Grace has been defined as "undeserved favor," and it is sufficient to cover all our sins. And the beautiful thing about grace is that God does not withdraw it when we stumble and fall; instead, He gently picks us up and enables us to take the next step.

At His throne of grace, we can always find the help we need. We can run to the Lord in times of trouble—when temptations beckon, when our hearts are breaking, at life's crossroads, and during the darkest of nights. Rest in this gift that God has so generously "poured out on us who belong to his dear Son." For His glorious grace abounds.

Father, as I consider my life—the things done and left undone—I'm so grateful for Your abounding grace.

JUNE 25

WE HAVE POWER

The Spirit of Him who raised Jesus from the dead dwells in [us].

ROMANS 8:11

Read today's verse again. Amid all the many promises in God's Word, this is an amazing truth. A power stronger than death is not a power to ignore, and when we accept Jesus as our Lord and choose to follow Him, that power is available to us.

God's Spirit "gives power to the weak" (Isaiah 40:29). He will also give us peace when we are overwhelmed, comfort when we are discouraged, rest when we are exhausted—mentally, physically, emotionally, and spiritually. We know from God's Word that His Spirit gives us the power to live each day whatever the circumstances. And we won't just live, we'll live abundantly, praising Him, shining His light, and sharing His love.

Lord God, teach me to tap into the power of Your Spirit for strength, for energy, for guidance, for comfort.

JUNE 26

WHEN WE'RE FEARFUL

The Lord stood with me and strengthened me.

2 TIMOTHY 4:17

The Lord calls us to keep our eyes on Him throughout life's journey. He has promised to provide all we need, including strength, wisdom, and guidance. But God's enemy and ours—Satan himself—will whisper in our ears to stir up fear instead of faith.

Fear can shift our focus from God to self. Fear can draw us inward, distance us from the Lord, and deafen us to the leading of the Holy Spirit. Our hearts and minds then become temptation's playground, and we can even begin to doubt our relationship with our heavenly Father. God's truth, set forth in His Word, shines its bright light on the enemy's lies. Open its pages and let God's perfect love—evident from Genesis through Revelation—cast out all fear as you keep your eyes on Him.

Lord, shield me from the lies and temptations of the evil one. Guard me with the truth of Your Word.

JUNE 27

CHRIST RECEIVES US

Receive one another, just as Christ also received us, to the glory of God.

ROMANS 15:7

It's a sin so commonplace in our world that it can easily slip into our churches, even into our own hearts if we aren't careful. What is it? It goes by a few different names—favoritism, partiality, discrimination. But no matter what you call it, God has this to say about it: "If you show partiality, you commit sin, and are convicted by the law as transgressors" (James 2:9).

Why does God so definitely condemn so common a sin? Because God Himself invites *everyone* to come to Him—and He richly welcomes *all* who choose to follow Him. Who are we to turn away people God welcomes? Because of the clothes they wear, the color of their skin, or the houses they live in—or don't live in? "Receive one another." Because God promises to graciously and lovingly receive you.

Lord, help me see as You see—with a heart of love for all.

JUNE 28

USE YOUR IMPATIENCE

Rest in the Lord, and wait patiently for Him; do not fret because of him who prospers in his way.

PSALM 37:7

Whether we're feeling impatient with a person, a trial, or even God Himself, we must remember that He is sovereign, which means that those people and situations didn't just randomly fall into our lives. At the very least, they give us an opportunity to look to God, draw upon His wisdom and strength, and grow in His grace.

When impatience causes you frustration, ask your heavenly Father to give you the patience you need—patience He wants to give you. Find an appropriate promise from Scripture and write it on your heart. Then trust that God will use whatever person or situation is making you feel impatient to make you more like His Son. Use your impatience to draw closer to the Lord.

Lord, as frustrating situations arise, remind me to use them as a chance to grow closer to You.

JUNE 29

ROBE OF RIGHTEOUSNESS

He has clothed me with the garments of salvation, He has covered me with the robe of righteousness.

ISAIAH 61:10

Jesus was the perfect Lamb of God, unblemished by sin, wholly divine and wholly human. He alone was qualified to be the once-for-all sacrifice for humanity's sins. But listen to this beautiful truth: our sovereign and gracious God clothes *us* with Jesus' righteousness. He takes our filthy rags of sin and replaces them with "garments of salvation."

There is absolutely nothing we sinners can do to cleanse ourselves of our sin or to bridge the immeasurable gap between us and our holy God. When we choose to accept His divine arrangement, though, we are made righteous not because of who we are or what we've done, but only because God chooses to accept Jesus' sacrifice . . . and then lovingly bestow His righteousness on us.

Father God, thank You for removing my rags and covering me with Your robe of righteousness.

JUNE 30

HE WILL RESTORE YOU

"You have gone away from My ordinances and have not kept them. Return to Me, and I will return to you," says the Lord of hosts.

MALACHI 3:7

Are you feeling a bit complacent about your relationship with Jesus? Have life's demands or hurts put your spiritual health on the back burner? Are you just going through the motions of following Jesus? Are you so distracted or burdened that you're hardly even following Him at all?

Your *yes* to any of these questions is actually an encouraging sign of self-awareness and your dissatisfaction with the spiritual status quo. For a fresh start right now, confess to God your need for Him. Open your Bible, and let His truth wash over you and renew your heart and mind. Ask God to reenergize your passion for Him, and recommit to making Him a priority in your life.

It's a wonderful promise: if we return to Him, He will always return to us.

Lord, thank You for Your faithfulness. Restore me to a thriving relationship with You.

JULY

JULY 1

WE'LL BE HOLY

Let us cleanse ourselves from everything that contaminates body and spirit, completing holiness [living a consecrated life—a life set apart for God's purpose] in the fear of God.

2 CORINTHIANS 7:1 AMP

We are not a naturally holy people, and there is nothing we can do to make ourselves holy. But God loves us so much that He is willing to make us holy, so that we can be with Him. How? His Word tells us that we are "made holy by the sacrifice of the body of Jesus Christ" (Hebrews 10:10 NLT). Our holiness begins by accepting that Jesus is our one and only Savior.

Then we must "cleanse ourselves from everything that contaminates body and spirit." We must disconnect ourselves from the unholy things of this world. As we choose to live daily in the presence of Christ, set apart for Him and for heaven, we will be made pure by His promises.

Father, thank You for the gift of Your Son, whose loving sacrifice makes me holy.

JULY 2

THE ANGEL STAYS NEAR

"Behold, I send an Angel before you to keep you in the way and to bring you into the place which I have prepared."

EXODUS 23:20

The Israelites, so recently escaped from slavery in Egypt, traveled toward the promised land. But God did not leave them to finish their journey alone. He sent His angel "to keep [them] in the way and to bring [them] into the place which I have prepared."

In the same way, God rescues us from our slavery to sin, but He does not then abandon us to complete the journey to heaven on our own. He sends His Spirit to keep us on the path He has prepared for us. We have a Guide to help us avoid the snares of life and a powerful Protector to shield us from those who seek to harm us. "The angel of the LORD encamps all around those who fear Him, and delivers them" (Psalm 34:7).

Father, I pray that I will be sensitive to the leading and voice of Your Spirit. Guide and protect me this day.

GOD'S WORD SECURES US

If you receive my words, and treasure my commands within you . . . then you will understand the fear of the L*ORD*, *and find the knowledge of God.*

PROVERBS 2:1, 5

The more we know and understand God's Word, the more secure we can feel in our walk with God. But so many times we fail to seek God's wisdom in His Word before we act; we strive to satisfy our desires without regard to the future or the consequences.

In this life, tests will come in all shapes and sizes. Some will require us to endure. Some we will anticipate, while others will blindside us. All of them ask us to make the right decisions. Regardless of the test, God instructs us to come to Him for the wisdom we so desperately need (James 1:5). Then we'll "understand the fear of the LORD" and know our secure place in His care.

Lord, open Your Word to me and wrap me in the security of its truths.

JULY 4

GET FREE

"If you abide in My word, you are My disciples indeed. And you shall know the truth, and the truth shall make you free."

JOHN 8:31–32

"You shall know the truth, and the truth shall make you free"—that is the promise given to the disciples of Jesus. When Jesus spoke these words to the Jews, they did not understand, saying, "We are Abraham's descendants, and have never been in bondage to anyone. How can You say, 'You will be made free'?" (v. 33). But Jesus wasn't speaking of the slavery of one man to another; He was speaking of their—and our—slavery to sin.

No matter how hard we try to live good and sinless lives, we will all fail at times. But when Jesus died upon the cross, He took away the authority of sin to enslave us. If we will believe the truth of who He is and what He did for us, that truth will set us free from the burden of our sins.

Lord Jesus, only You can set me free. Forgive me, cleanse me, make me Your own.

JULY 5

GOD'S PROMISE

"I set My rainbow in the cloud, and it shall be for the sign of the covenant between Me and the earth."

GENESIS 9:13

God never turns His back on those He created. Regardless of how thoroughly we have infected our lives with sin, He still seeks a way to save us from ourselves. Consider Noah. The world Noah lived in was filled with people whose every thought was corrupted. "But Noah found grace in the eyes of the Lord" (Genesis 6:8). So when the Flood came and all was destroyed, God saved Noah. Then He set the rainbow in the sky as a sign to His faithful servant—and to us.

The rainbow not only reminds us that God will never again flood the earth; it reminds us that ours is a God of incredible majesty and might. The next time a rainbow shines across the sky, remember that our God keeps His promises.

Father, You were faithful to save Noah, and I know You will be faithful to save me.

JULY 6

GOD'S LOVE HEALS

To you who fear My name the Sun of Righteousness shall arise with healing in His wings.

MALACHI 4:2

It makes total sense that the God who created us can also heal us physically, mentally, emotionally, and spiritually. Our Creator God is our Great Physician as well.

We should thank God for His restorative power and never hesitate to ask Him for His healing touch whenever we are hurting. Whatever the source and whatever the site of our pain, whether we are physically ill, brokenhearted by a relationship, or overwhelmed by the demands of life, we can experience the Lord as our great Comforter. He knows our every tear (Psalm 56:8).

Our God is Jehovah, the great and mighty Healer. His love for us is everlasting, and when we cry out to Him in fear or distress, He comes to us "with healing in His wings."

Lord, You are Comforter, Physician, Redeemer—I rest in the healing of Your unconditional love.

JULY 7

GOD'S PROMISE OF BLESSING

"If you walk in My statutes and keep My commandments, and perform them. . . . You shall eat your bread to the full, and dwell in your land safely."

LEVITICUS 26:3, 5

In Leviticus 26, the Lord guaranteed some blessings to the Israelites, His chosen people. Their land would be fruitful (vv. 3–4), they would have plenty to eat (v. 5), and their enemies would be utterly defeated (vv. 7–8). He would be their God and they would be His people (v. 12). They had only to keep His commands.

The Lord offers us even greater blessings if we keep His commands. When we put Him first in our lives, when we live so that the light of His love shines through us for all the world to see, God's blessings to us are far more wonderful than any worldly riches and security. For God promises us forgiveness of our sins and His presence, both now and later in heaven.

Lord, bless me that I might bless others with the love You so richly give to me.

JULY 8

GOD KEEPS HIS PROMISES

Every good word which the Lord your God spoke and promised to you has been fulfilled for you.

JOSHUA 23:15 AMP

In this passage, Joshua reminded the Israelites of the faithfulness of God in fulfilling His promises—Jericho's walls really did fall down, Israel's enemies really did falter, and the promised land really was theirs. God keeps His promises.

Now, couple that fact with this truth: God never changes (James 1:17). So what does that tell us about the promises God gives to us? He will keep them, every last one. When we choose to become followers of God, He really will forgive us; He really will help and uphold us, guide and strengthen, protect and shield us; and He really will take us home to heaven with Him.

Because God keeps His promises.

Lord, I thank You for all Your promises, but especially for Your faithfulness—I always trust You to do what You say.

JULY 9

COURAGE WHEN WE NEED IT

"Go! I will be with you as you speak, and I will instruct you in what to say."

EXODUS 4:12 NLT

At times, we may be absolutely sure about what we need to do, but we're afraid—as Moses was when God sent him to demand that Pharaoh let the Israelites go free. Other times we are confident that God is nudging us to speak certain words or make a specific decision, but we lack the courage to step out in faith. When we feel nervous about doing God's will, we must trust Him to give us the courage we need. Because He will.

As we prayerfully take the first step, we'll experience God's power. Our heavenly Father will give us strength for every situation we face, just as He gave Moses all he needed to lead the Israelites to freedom. When we rely on God's power, we will be able to put aside fear. That is God's promise to us, His children.

Lord, help me sense Your gentle nudgings, then fill me with the courage to do whatever You ask of me.

JULY 10

FULL OF GOD HIMSELF

I bow my knees to the Father of our Lord Jesus Christ, . . . that you may be filled with all the fullness of God.

EPHESIANS 3:14, 19

Growing in your knowledge of the Lord Jesus Christ is essential to your walk with God. He wants you to learn continually about Him and His Son, Jesus, throughout your life. But walking closely with God and in His knowledge and wisdom happens only when you read God's Word. Not a cursory, just-on-Sunday-morning kind of reading, but a one-on-one meeting with God in His Word. As you come to know Your Lord better, you'll more clearly hear His voice, more easily respond to His leading. And following Him—obeying His commands and walking according to His ways—will bless you as well as glorify Him.

Your desire to grow spiritually is very much in line with God's will, and as you do your part, He will do His: He will fill you "with all the fullness of God."

Lord, I pray that You would fill me up with Your words, Your truths, Your love.

JULY 11

THE SPIRIT LEADS TO LIFE

If by the Spirit you put to death the deeds of the body, you will live. For as many as are led by the Spirit of God, these are sons of God.

ROMANS 8:13–14

When we choose to follow Jesus, we step away from our self-driven lives and agree to begin living God-driven lives. We can do this because of the grace of God—grace that was purchased with the sacrifice of His own Son.

Grace does not erase the power of sin to harm us. There are always consequences for our sins, but grace does give us the Holy Spirit. And we can count on His help to turn away from our self-centered lives. He will shield us from the evil one and guide us through this life and home to heaven. As we turn to Him, seeking His light to illuminate our path, and as we listen to His voice as He tells us which way to go, the Spirit leads us to eternal life.

Lord, I choose to walk away from my own selfish desires and be led by Your Spirit.

JULY 12

PERPLEXED BUT HOPEFUL

We are hard-pressed on every side, yet not crushed; we are perplexed, but not in despair; persecuted, but not forsaken; struck down, but not destroyed.

2 CORINTHIANS 4:8–9

Disappointment is a part of life—and not one of us is immune to its effects. So when life brings its letdowns, the best comfort is in the arms of our heavenly Father. He provides reassurance no other source can. And the good news is, He promises to save us, revive us, and "perfect that which concerns [us]" (Psalm 138:8). He does not abandon us during difficult times.

It's important to acknowledge and grieve disappointments when they come, but it's also important to move forward by finding comfort in God's promises of hope and joy. These promises transcend this world and its heartache. He is always ready to console and encourage us.

Lord, surround me with Your presence and remind me of the joy of Your promises.

JULY 13

LIVE TO PLEASE GOD

"Just as you want men to do to you, you also do to them likewise."

LUKE 6:31

Many in our world today look at the golden rule and scoff, "That's insane! What's in it for *me*?"

The selfish desire to have our own way in life creates a wall between man and God. But the Lord encourages, "Love your enemies, do good, and lend, hoping for nothing in return; and your reward will be great" (v. 35)—the exact opposite of what the world encourages. The attitude we choose to embrace in our lives determines the kind of persons we become. God knows us from the inside out—and He also knows who we can be if we walk in His ways.

Let the chief desire of your heart be to please Him, and you will find that the way you walk and talk will help others see the love of Christ. Living to please God by treating others well will change everything.

Lord, fill me with a desire to put others first and to see service as an opportunity to share Your love.

JULY 14

CHANGELESS PROMISES

To Abraham and his Seed were the promises made.

GALATIANS 3:16

We think of God's promise to Abraham as the birth of Isaac and all the descendants who would come from him—more numerous than the stars (Genesis 22:17). But God's promise was "to Abraham and his Seed." That Seed is Christ. Jesus would come through Abraham to save us from our sins. God's keeping of that promise did not depend on the works of Abraham; it depended on the faithfulness of God.

More than four centuries passed between the promise to Abraham and the law of Moses. The law neither altered nor hindered the promise God made to save us. Salvation did not and does not come through our obedience. Salvation comes through faith in Christ, as was promised to Abraham . . . and to us.

Lord, I'm so grateful my salvation does not depend on how perfectly I obey. Thank You for Your saving grace.

JULY 15

CONSTANT COMPANION

There is a friend who sticks closer than a brother.

PROVERBS 18:24

David praised God for His constant presence in his life: "You go before me and follow me. You place your hand of blessing on my head" (Psalm 139:5 NLT). When Jesus came, He gave this promise: "I will never leave you nor forsake you" (Hebrews 13:5). And when the Holy Spirit came, Paul wrote: "Your body is the temple of the Holy Spirit who is in you" (1 Corinthians 6:19).

All that is to say that the full force of the Trinity is active in our lives: The Lord God watches over us. Jesus walks beside us. And the Spirit dwells within us.

Once we name Jesus as our Savior and Lord, we are never alone. Not for an instant are we left without help or without hope. We have a constant Companion.

Lord, thank You for Your constant presence.
Fill my life with Yourself, O Lord.

JULY 16

A LEGACY OF INTEGRITY

The righteous man walks in his integrity;
his children are blessed after him.

PROVERBS 20:7

Integrity: it is such an important word. It helps describe who we are in the Lord and how we are seen by those we live, work, and serve with. It is the foundation of the lives we lead and an essential element in our relationship with our heavenly Father.

The Lord calls each of us to do what is good and right, to live according to His Word, because godly living reflects His holy character and gives glory to Him. If you choose to walk in God's way and become a person of integrity, God will make you a blessing to all those around you. Your life will be transformed into a gift and an example that lasts for generations. It would be difficult to think of a greater legacy to leave your loved ones than a personal record of godly, faithful integrity.

Lord, teach me to live a life of integrity—a praise to You and a legacy to those I love.

JULY 17

A TEACHABLE HEART

If you listen to correction, you grow in understanding.

PROVERBS 15:32 NLT

When did you realize you don't actually know everything? The realization that you still have much to learn means becoming a lifelong student. And when you are a student of God, He promises to reveal Himself to you through His Word and Spirit (2 Timothy 3:16; 1 Corinthians 2:10).

Romans 12:2 encourages, "Let God transform you into a new person by changing the way you think" (NLT). God does not expect you simply to try harder or just sin less, but rather to learn from His instruction and correction and to depend on His Spirit. If you are teachable, God promises you will "grow in understanding." Then your heart "will be flooded with light" (Ephesians 1:18 NLT). God doesn't expect you to know everything—and what a relief—He just wants you to be willing to learn. God blesses a teachable heart.

Lord, teach me more and more
and more all the days of my life.

JULY 18

CHOSEN TO BEAR FRUIT

"I chose you and appointed you that you should go and bear fruit, and that your fruit should remain."

JOHN 15:16

Jesus does not want any of us to lead unproductive or unfocused lives. He chose us not only for salvation but also to play a significant role in His kingdom. He wants each of us to fulfill a particular purpose for our success and His glory.

We are designed to bear much fruit—to reflect God's love and character to the world. When our lives are filled with His purpose, we can do all the things He calls us to do through the strength of Christ (Philippians 4:13). God, through Paul, gave us this promise in Colossians: "Your lives will produce every kind of good fruit" (1:10 NLT). We are chosen for a reason: for salvation, yes, but also to bear lasting spiritual fruit and draw others to know God.

Lord, thank You for choosing me. Help me live a life bursting with Your spiritual fruit.

JULY 19

BE SUCCESSFUL

"Be careful to obey all the instructions Moses gave you. . . . Then you will be successful in everything you do."

JOSHUA 1:7 NLT

When we do God's will in God's way and with God's help, no one and nothing can stand in the way of our success. The key is the presence of the Lord. God commanded Joshua to meditate on His Word day and night (v. 8), and He is asking us to do the same today. He wants each of us to enjoy fruitful work and family life. Yet godly success may or may not look like worldly success. Our heavenly Father wants us to remember that our true treasures are the ones that accumulate in heaven.

When we discover the wisdom of God's Word and His way and apply it to our lives, everything changes. Our focus, priorities, emotions, and hearts become God-centered. Then we will receive God's richest rewards of peace, guidance, salvation, and an eternity spent with Him. *That* is true and lasting success.

Father, please teach me the true definition of success and fill my life with godly treasures.

JULY 20

MORE PRECIOUS THAN GOLD

How much better to get wisdom than gold! And to get understanding is to be chosen rather than silver.

PROVERBS 16:16

The love of money touches everyone in some way, and we can easily find ourselves spending most of our waking hours chasing riches: the more we get, the more we seem to want.

The Bible condemns the unchecked desire to get rich (1 Timothy 6:9), not because money is a sin, but because money makes a terrible master. Jesus told us, "No one can serve two masters. For you will hate one and love the other. . . . You cannot serve God and be enslaved to money" (Matthew 6:24 NLT). We must guard against allowing money to become our master. Instead, we must seek to serve the one true Master in every area of our lives. When we do, He promises to bless us with all the riches of heaven (Philippians 4:19).

Father, deliver me from a love of money and fill my heart with the desire to seek You.

JULY 21

PRAYER ACCOMPLISHES MUCH

Pray for one another, that you may be healed. The effective, fervent prayer of a righteous man avails much.

JAMES 5:16

Someone has said that prayer is like the breath of life: you cannot exist spiritually without it. It binds us to our fellow believers as we lift them up to our Lord and they do the same for us. It also binds us to God as we humbly bow our hearts before Him and seek His face.

When we go to God in earnest prayer, seeking His will and earnestly baring our souls for God's direction, our lives are changed and God is glorified. Prayer is no small thing. It is the very breath of our spiritual lives, and our Father promises that our prayers accomplish much in this world.

Father, I bow before You, surrender to You.
Hear the prayers of my heart.

JULY 22

GOD BLESSES THE THANKFUL

Blessed be the Lord, who daily loads us with benefits, the God of our salvation!

PSALM 68:19

Can we even begin to number the benefits and blessings we receive from the Lord? We've come to expect so many of these daily things of life. Of course we remember to thank God for the big things—for answered prayers, for salvation. But do we remember to give thanks for His countless daily blessings?

Have we thanked Him for the dawning of a new day? For the warmth of our bed or the morning's first steaming cup of coffee? For our spouse's hug, our child's smile, our friend's caring call? Do we remember the One who taught that bird outside our window to sing and gave it its song? Every breath of every moment is filled with the promised blessings of God—if we but open our eyes to see them. Thank Him for *all* His benefits today.

Father, I am so grateful for Your blessings—
open my eyes to see each one.

JULY 23

WHEN WE PURSUE GOD

In every work that [King Hezekiah] began in the service of the house of God, in the law and in the commandment, to seek his God, he did it with all his heart. So he prospered.

2 CHRONICLES 31:21

True devotion to God changes you from the inside out, first turning your heart toward the Lord. As the heart changes and pleasing God becomes a priority in your life, your behavior also changes. And despite what the world likes to proclaim, obedience to the Lord brings more pleasure, more joy than does any sin.

When you seek the Lord with all your heart, He promises that you will find Him (Jeremiah 29:13). The natural result of finding Him is a joyful and earnest obedience to His will. That obedience will open your life to all the blessings of God—peace, love, joy, wisdom, strength, encouragement, and so much more—both in this world and in your eternal heavenly home.

Lord, I seek to know and serve You with all my heart. Help me to be obedient in all my ways.

JULY 24

OUR FAITH WILL GROW

Like newborn babies, crave pure spiritual milk, so that by it you may grow up in your salvation.

1 PETER 2:2 NIV

Back in the thirteenth century, Richard of Chichester prayed that he would "see thee more clearly, love thee more dearly, and follow thee more nearly." This timeless prayer captures the essence of a Christ-centered life: we are to continually grow in knowledge, in understanding, in wisdom.

For the Christian that is no arduous task. Once we taste the goodness, the graciousness, and the kindness of God, we cannot help but crave more.

Make some time every day to be alone, read the Bible, think about what you read, and pray. God will bless you in those times, even as He uses them to grow your faith and prepare you for future service to His people and in the world.

Lead me, Lord, to see You more clearly, love You more dearly, and follow You more nearly, each day of my life.

JULY 25

GOD IS LOVE

Beloved, let us love one another, for love is of God; and everyone who loves is born of God and knows God. He who does not love does not know God, for God is love.

1 JOHN 4:7–8

God is love. It's who He is, and it's what He does. And love is what He commands us to do. More than that, love is what defines us as belonging to Him. To "love one another" is our charge from God, not as an odious obligation that must be fulfilled, but as an expression of gratitude so deep that we cannot help but do as He asks. Even when it's not easy; even when it's downright hard.

So what is God's kind of love? It is action, not just feeling. It is patient and kind. It does not envy or boast. It isn't proud or self-seeking or easily angered. It always protects, trusts, hopes, and perseveres (1 Corinthians 13:4–7).

That is how we should love others because that is how God promises to love us.

Love defines who You are, Lord. Let it define me too.

JULY 26

HARMONY AND PEACE

The wisdom that is from above is first pure, then peaceable, gentle, willing to yield, full of mercy and good fruits, without partiality and without hypocrisy.

JAMES 3:17

You have heard the expression *You are what you eat*. We might also say we reflect the ideas and principles we consume. Worldly principles and ideas are destructive, harsh, full of critical judgment and hypocrisy. But James tells us that God's wisdom is just the opposite—full of gentleness, mercy, kindness, and impartiality.

While worldly wisdom leads to factions, bitterness, and dissension, godly wisdom leads to harmony, peace, and positive relationships. Take a look at your own intake: What wisdom are you seeking? What ideas are you embracing? Remember, you will become what you consume. Choose wisely. And He will bless you.

Lord, lead my heart and mind to seek Your wisdom; shield me from the wisdom of this world.

JULY 27

BIG ENOUGH

He stirs up the sea with His power, and by His understanding He breaks up the storm.

JOB 26:12

We use the words *Lord*, *God*, *King*, sprinkling them into prayers and praises. But how often do we stop and think about who God *really* is?

He's the One who hung the earth on *nothing*. He gathers up the waters and binds them into clouds. He alone tells the light where to end and the darkness where to begin. He stirs up seas, breaks up storms, and adorns the heavens (vv. 7–13). But even all this reflects just "the mere edges of His ways, and how small a whisper we hear of Him!" (v. 14).

Who dares to declare a limit to His power? And what does that power mean for us? It means that whatever winds whip at the borders of our lives, whatever storms surge through—our God is big enough to say, "Peace, be still!" (Mark 4:39). And He's loving enough to do it.

Lord, I trust You to be mighty enough to handle whatever comes my way.

JULY 28

JESUS IS OVER ALL

I am convinced that nothing can ever separate us from God's love.

ROMANS 8:38 NLT

We worry. We live in a human world where love seems to come and go, ebb and flow, start and stop. So we wonder: Will God ever stop loving me? Just listen to His resounding *no* as it's spelled out in verses 38–39: "Neither death nor life" is strong enough to break the bonds of God's love. No angels or demons, no government forces or powers can ever stand between us and Him. No past, present, or future sins, anxieties, or fears can dim His love for us. Nothing—no, nothing—not in the heights of the heavens or the depths of hell can separate us from love of our God.

Because all heaven and earth are under Jesus' authority (Matthew 28:18), and because He declared God's love for us in His sacrifice (John 3:16), God promises we can stop worrying about His love. It is ours . . . always.

Lord Jesus, thank You for gifting me with a love so great. Hold me ever close to You.

JULY 29

WE CAN KNOW GOD

"I will betroth you to Me in faithfulness,
and you shall know the Lord*."*

HOSEA 2:20

It's easy to know *about* God. We can read His Word. We can study commentaries and websites and cross-references. We can memorize who begat whom, which kings followed God, and which followed Baal. We can know what God said to Abraham and what Jesus said to Judas. We can know many things, and it is good to know about God.

But it is better to *know God* Himself. Our God does not hide Himself from us. In His Word, He has poured out the truth of who He is and what His will for us is. And to those who choose to follow Him, God sends His own Spirit to live inside us and open up the riches of His Word to us. When we join our lives to Him—through His Son, through prayer, through His Word—He promises that "[we] shall know the Lord."

I want to know You better, Lord. Please reveal Yourself to me through Your Word and Spirit.

JULY 30

FORGIVENESS OF SIN

In Him we have redemption through His blood, the forgiveness of sins, according to the riches of His grace.

EPHESIANS 1:7

We often use the words *redemption* and *forgiveness* interchangeably—as if they mean the same thing. But they do not. Christ first had to *redeem* us—to purchase our freedom from slavery to sin. A price had to be paid, and the price was the blood of Jesus, the Son of God. After the redeeming ransom was paid, then came the *forgiveness* of our sins: the washing away of all our wrongs. And that forgiveness was completed "according to the riches of His grace," which means we were not forgiven for *a* sin, but for all our sins—past, present, and future.

Because God's love and grace are so rich and unending, both redemption and forgiveness are offered to *all* . . . given to all who believe.

Lord Jesus, praise isn't enough;
I give You my life, my all.

JULY 31

WHAT MANNER OF LOVE

Behold what manner of love the Father has bestowed on us, that we should be called children of God!

1 JOHN 3:1

Often the hurt we feel in life results from an unexpected incident, an unanticipated turn of events, an unwanted change. And sometimes it's the result of a poor decision we've made that brings on shame and even doubt about God's love for us. In these stormy waters of life, though, cling to this lifeline of truth: you are God's own child, and His love for you will not diminish—no matter what.

God has loved you since He knit you together in your mother's womb, and He will love you for all of eternity. Nothing you do or say could ever make Him love you less or more. He already loves you perfectly. The God of the universe—who numbers each hair on your head—is critically invested in His relationship with you. What manner of love is this? It's God's love . . . for you.

Lord, You love me . . . still. Thank You, Lord.

AUGUST

AUGUST 1

ABUNDANT MERCY

He will abundantly pardon. . . . You shall go out with joy, and be led out with peace.

ISAIAH 55:7, 12

When we seek God's presence, He will be there. And those who seek the Lord, who daily turn to Him, find that He is gracious and will "abundantly pardon" all their failures. But more than that, He leads us along the pathways to the bountiful life He has planned for us.

Even when we don't understand what God is doing in our lives or in our world (which may happen frequently), we can trust Him. He has a plan, and it is perfect. And when we choose to keep walking with Him, He will bless us with His promised mercy and abundant life, joy, and peace.

Lord, please wash me with Your mercies and lead me into the life You have planned for me.

AUGUST 2

THE PROMISE OF GOODNESS

"The people of the world will see all the good I do for my people, and they will tremble with awe at the peace and prosperity I provide for them."

JEREMIAH 33:9 NLT

Many people have a wrong idea about God. They see Him as some coldhearted character just waiting in heaven for us to sin, so that He can rain down wrath and punishment. That is not God. Our God is good. He is love. And what He is waiting for is our decision to follow Him—so that He can shower us with kindness.

We access God's kindness by seeking Him, casting our cares upon Him, and receiving His peace. With the Lord, we can exchange our weariness for His strength, our confusion for His wisdom, our fears for His courage. God's goodness comes into our lives when we are willing to follow Him. We then receive His promised blessings of "peace and prosperity"—transforming our lives into a beautiful witness for Him.

Lord, please fill my life with Your kindness—and teach me to share it with others.

AUGUST 3

GOD EXPLAINS THE WAY

"Come now, and let us reason together," says the Lord, *"though your sins are like scarlet, they shall be as white as snow."*

ISAIAH 1:18

God's message is not a complicated one. Over and over, in His New Testament covenant, God tells us that the way to heaven—to peace, love, joy, mercy, and grace—is through a personal relationship with Him, made possible by the sacrifice of His Son. While it's true we cannot fully understand all the whys and the hows of salvation, we *can* understand the way. Perhaps Peter said it best. When the people asked how they must be saved, he replied, "Repent, and let every one of you be baptized in the name of Jesus Christ for the remission of sins; and you shall receive the gift of the Holy Spirit" (Acts 2:38).

God does not hide His path from us. "Come now, and let us reason together," He says. *Let Me explain the way.* And then He promises, "though your sins are like scarlet, they shall be as white as snow."

Father, with Your words, You show me the way. Help me follow as You lead.

AUGUST 4

THE LORD WON'T FORGET US

"I will not forget you. See, I have inscribed you on the palms of My hands."

ISAIAH 49:15–16

Do you ever feel forgotten by the world? Invisible? The world just seems to keep rushing right along, as if you aren't even standing there, hurting and wounded.

At times, we might even feel abandoned and forgotten by God. When everything is going wrong, when our prayers seem to be met with silence, we can feel invisible even to our all-knowing God.

But we aren't. God never forgets us, never abandons us. He could no more abandon His children than a nursing mother could forget her child (v. 15). Our Lord hears our every cry, every prayer. And He is walking beside us through whatever troubles we face. "I will not forget you," He promises—and God always keeps His word.

I know, Lord, that Your presence and Your care are with me always. Thank You.

AUGUST 5

THE GREAT PHYSICIAN HEALS

Heal me, O LORD, and I shall be healed; save me, and I shall be saved, for You are my praise.

JEREMIAH 17:14

It can be argued that the best place to begin any battle is on your knees—whether it's a battle for your health, your family, your home, or your soul. When you draw near to God in prayer, you will find healing for your spirit, body, and life. Listen, meditate, and wait for His direction and guidance.

God wants the best for you, and the best is to walk closely with Him, trusting Him in every situation and relationship. James 4:7 says, "Submit to God. Resist the devil and he will flee from you." God is asking you to take the first step. The Great Physician stands waiting with open arms to make you whole. Do not hesitate. Run to Him for everything you need today.

Father God, You are the Great Physician. Heal me. Make me whole and wholly Yours.

AUGUST 6

UNDER GOD'S PROTECTION

"No weapon formed against you shall prosper, and every tongue which rises against you in judgment you shall condemn. This is the heritage of the servants of the Lord."

ISAIAH 54:17

There is no weapon, God said, that can defeat His people—neither one forged from steel nor one welded with words. This promise God made to the people of Israel stills hold true for us today. It is our guarantee of victory over evil, our "heritage" as "servants of the Lord."

When we dedicate our lives to God, when we walk daily by His side, He becomes our Rock, our Shield, our Deliverer (Psalm 18:2). When we call upon Him, we are saved from our enemies (Psalm 18:3). God's desire is for His children to live in the pleasure of His love and grace. So He stands as our Defender, protecting us from all foes, weapons, and adversaries.

Lord, protect me from those who do evil;
shelter me with Your love and grace.

AUGUST 7

JESUS PAID IT ALL

Adam's one sin brings condemnation for everyone, but Christ's one act of righteousness brings a right relationship with God.

ROMANS 5:18 NLT

Because of the sin of Adam, all of humanity owes a debt to God so huge that we could never hope to repay it. That debt condemns us to spiritual death and an eternity of separation from God.

But then Jesus came. His death on the cross changed everything. For just "as by one man's disobedience many were made sinners, so also by one Man's obedience many will be made righteous" (v. 19). Jesus took our punishment and gave us His righteousness. As His followers, we are not only released from death's hold, we are lifted up as coheirs of Christ to live forever in heaven.

We no longer owe a debt for our sins. Jesus paid it all.

Lord Jesus, You paid all I could never pay.
Make my life a living praise to You.

AUGUST 8

JUSTIFIED AND GLORIFIED

Whom He predestined, these He also called; whom He called, these He also justified; and whom He justified, these He also glorified.

ROMANS 8:30

God knows everyone who will ever be born and everyone who has already been born. And in one of those great, mind-boggling mysteries of the power of God, He also knows who will answer His call and who will not.

God's knowledge does not rob us of our free will; rather He simply already knows who will choose Him. All are called and all are wanted, but not all choose to come.

Those who do answer His call are justified; we are "declared free of the guilt of sin" (v. 30 AMP). And we who are justified are also glorified, transformed into the image of Christ, and raised up "to a heavenly dignity" (v. 30 AMP).

Father, I praise You for knowing—for justifying and transforming—me.

AUGUST 9

YOU'VE GOT TALENT

"I have filled him with the Spirit of God, giving him great wisdom, ability, and expertise in all kinds of crafts."

EXODUS 31:3 NLT

Did you know that you have been given powerful influence over those who surround you at work, at church, and in your home? God, in His divine mercy and infinite wisdom, has given you certain gifts and talents. And how you use them will determine the effect you have on those you love and work with.

Will you use your talents for your own selfish gain or for the good of all? To tear others down or lift them up? To bring glory and fame to your own name or to share the love of God? In His Word, God tells us that gifts are given so that "we can help each other" (1 Corinthians 12:7 NLT) and "serve one another" (1 Peter 4:10 NLT). When we faithfully use the gifts God has given us, He promises to bless us with even more (Luke 16:10).

Father, please show me the gifts You've given me—and how I can use them to honor You.

AUGUST 10

CHRIST IS THE ANSWER

"The Lord has anointed Me . . . to heal the brokenhearted, to proclaim liberty to the captives, and the opening of the prison to those who are bound."

ISAIAH 61:1

It wasn't long after Jesus faced the devil in the desert that He faced the doubters in His own hometown. Standing in the synagogue at Nazareth, Jesus read from the passage we now know as Isaiah 61:1–2. When He had finished, He said, "Today this Scripture is fulfilled in your hearing" (Luke 4:21).

At first, the crowd "marveled" at His words (v. 22). But when Jesus spoke of God's blessings being offered to all—not just the Israelites—the crowd was "filled with wrath" and tried to throw Him off a cliff (vv. 28–29).

But Jesus spoke truth. He is the answer—for all people, for all heartaches, troubles, and fears. Jesus is our answer!

Jesus, teach me to turn to You and to listen for Your voice.

AUGUST 11

GOD WILL HELP US DISCERN

Do not believe every spirit, but test the spirits, whether they are of God. . . . Every spirit that confesses that Jesus Christ has come in the flesh is of God.

1 JOHN 4:1–2

The apostle John warns us not to believe every spirit—some of them lie. They lie through false teachers and false writings. We simply cannot trust everything we hear. Some people claim to be Christians, but the message they teach is wholly different from the message of Christ. There are many false prophets at work, so we must test every message to see whether it truly is from God.

We must compare everything we hear to the absolute truth of God's Word. It's the sword that cuts through all the lies (Hebrews 4:12). And we must listen to the Holy Spirit, who also helps us discern what is truth. Remember, Jesus is the *only* way to God; let no one tell you different.

Lord, please shield me from those who try to lead me away from You.

AUGUST 12

AS YOU BLESS, BE BLESSED

Honor the Lord with your possessions, and with the firstfruits of all your increase; so your barns will be filled with plenty, and your vats will overflow with new wine.

PROVERBS 3:9–10

Everything belongs to God. When we realize that our things are not really our own, it is much easier to share them. Just as He graciously gives us good things every day, we should look for ways to bless others, demonstrating to the world the boundless love of God. When we choose to honor God with all we have and bless those who are struggling in life, we become true servants of our living God.

God is constantly watching over us, noting our decisions, pondering our plans, and observing our behavior. He invites us to ask Him for His counsel. As we bless others, He is waiting to bless us with His love and grace.

Father, I pray that my giving would reflect the love and gratitude I feel for all You have done for me.

AUGUST 13

GOD REWARDS OUR FAITH

Without faith it is impossible to please Him, for he who comes to God must believe that He is, and that He is a rewarder of those who diligently seek Him.

HEBREWS 11:6

Hebrews tells us that "faith is the substance of things hoped for, the evidence of things not seen" (v. 1). Faith is *not* dreaming or wishing or merely believing what you know logically cannot be true. Instead, it is the certainty that God's character is perfectly reliable.

Faith lets us admit our inadequacy—that we do not understand, that we cannot do it all on our own, that we do not know the way we should go—while also declaring the perfect wisdom, mighty power, and absolute dependability of God. When we diligently seek out the Lord in faith, believing He will do for us as His Word promises, God rewards us . . . blessing us with the fulfillment of those promises.

Lord, I do have faith, but please strengthen it.

AUGUST 14

GREATNESS IN SERVING

"The Son of Man came not to be served but to serve others and to give his life as a ransom for many."

MARK 10:45 NLT

The most honored in God's kingdom are characterized not by power or prestige but by humble service. Jesus expressed this truth when He told the disciples, "Whoever desires to become great among you shall be your servant" (v. 43).

Just imagine for a moment: Jesus left the greatness of heaven for a humble manger. He lived a life of near poverty, with no home of His own. He touched, He healed, He taught, He washed feet—yes, even the feet of His greatest betrayer. And then He sacrificed Himself to offer redemption to all who would accept it.

This beautiful verse from Mark illustrates the deep and sacrificial love of God—and the promised power to be found in serving others.

Lord Jesus, Your life is a picture of service.
Teach me to serve as You did.

AUGUST 15

THROUGH HIS WORD

I will never forget your commandments, for by them you give me life.

PSALM 119:93 NLT

Many Christians have never experienced the power and encouragement offered in memorizing Scripture. When we lock portions of God's Word in our minds and hearts, they remain available to help strengthen us in difficult times. We are able to meditate on them, ponder them, and apply them—whether we have our Bibles with us or not. And as we memorize His Word, we find that the Holy Spirit often calls those words to mind just when we need them most.

Living for Jesus is meant to be a full-time, twenty-four/seven experience. The more we allow the Word to be a part of our lives, the more we grow spiritually. God has given us the sword of the Spirit, which is the Word of God. Let's let life grow in us through His Word.

Lord, write Your Word not only upon my mind but also upon my heart, so it will ever be with me.

AUGUST 16

PRAISE GOD TOGETHER

Live in complete harmony with each other, as is fitting for followers of Christ Jesus. . . . Accept each other just as Christ has accepted you so that God will be given glory.

ROMANS 15:5, 7 NLT

Though as believers we all love and follow the same God, we too often get tangled up in our opinions over things that ultimately don't matter, such as which songs to praise our Lord with, what color carpet to put in the sanctuary, and whether Sunday school should happen before or after worship.

Disagreements in the church happened in Paul's day too, so he wrote Romans 15. His advice is just as applicable in the twenty-first century as it was in biblical times: let's allow God to teach us to love and get along with each other. As we accept and respect our brothers and sisters in Christ, we will bring Him glory. Let's praise Him together.

Lord, help me love my fellow believers as I love You.

AUGUST 17

DAILY RENEWAL

We do not lose heart. Even though our outward man is perishing, yet the inward man is being renewed day by day.

2 CORINTHIANS 4:16

Living for God from the inside out begins with a change of heart and your decision to be a different person. The way you walk, talk, and interact with people you encounter will change as you respond to the call to reflect Jesus in every area of your life.

When you become a Christian, you assume a personal responsibility to live for Christ. Although your sins have been forgiven through His sacrifice, you are still responsible for your behavior. What you do on earth matters. And while God doesn't demand perfection, pleasing Him is to be your first priority. This is possible because of the promise: "the inward man is being renewed day by day." This ongoing renewal empowers you to do good things as you live for God from the inside out.

Lord, thank You for renewing me, day by day, so that I may please You with my words, my actions, my life.

AUGUST 18

HE MAKES YOU ABLE

God is my strength and power, and He makes my way perfect.

2 SAMUEL 22:33

Whenever God allows you to experience more demands, setbacks, and even pain than you think you can handle, it's easy to become overwhelmed and find yourself discouraged. You may even wonder, *Why should I get up in the morning when the burdens are so heavy and the path ahead unclear?*

Why? Because it's in the seasons like these that your heavenly Father will draw you closest to Him. It's in these difficult times that you will experience the bittersweet joy of knowing He is your Rock. And He will enable you, by His power and His presence, to stand strong in every trial and to navigate every tribulation. Throughout the ages, God has been faithful to His people. He is faithful now, and He will be your strength for whatever problems you face.

Lord, when I am overwhelmed, remind me that You make me strong when I am weak—and You will make a way for me.

AUGUST 19

HINGED ON LOVE

Know that the LORD your God, He is God, the faithful God who keeps covenant and mercy for a thousand generations.

DEUTERONOMY 7:9

Everything you do and face is hinged on love, because God, who is love, created you in His image. When you pray and the Lord's answer is "Wait," it is because He loves you and knows you need time to grow into the plans He has for you. When the overwhelming choices before you make it hard to know which way is up, our Lord and Savior shows you your need to depend on His guiding love.

Until you come to understand at your deepest level that God is love, you will struggle with trusting Him, obeying Him, and seeking Him wholeheartedly. One of the keys to your spiritual growth is believing in God's love—believing He "keeps covenant and mercy for a thousand generations"—even when you can't see it.

Father, thank You for keeping Your promises and loving me continually.

AUGUST 20

GOD GIVES POWER

He never grows weak or weary. . . . He gives power to the weak and strength to the powerless.

ISAIAH 40:28–29 NLT

There are days—even weeks or months—when we are simply . . . tired. When we're not sure if we can take the next step, and we're not entirely certain we want to. Even when we feel paralyzed by exhaustion, we can drop to our knees and cry out, "I give everything to You, Lord."

He is mighty enough to handle whatever we give Him. "He never grows weak or weary." He always knows just what to do and to say. Not only is His strength unending, He generously shares it with us.

Hand over your cares to Him—and refuse to allow yourself to snatch them back to worry over on your own. Trust the One who "gives power to the weak."

Father, I feel so lost and so tired. Hold me, guide me, strengthen me.

AUGUST 21

PRAISE, GLORY, HONOR

When your faith remains strong through many trials, it will bring you much praise and glory and honor.

1 PETER 1:7 NLT

God knows you face difficult situations. He hears your cries. Even those who maintain the closest fellowship with Him are susceptible to feelings of hopelessness when problems seem insurmountable. Sometimes God allows you to face "impossible" circumstances to test your faith. When there is no other place to turn, you are forced to seek God, and in Him you will find the very answers you need.

God knows exactly the path to take to solve your problems and to bring you into a more intimate relationship with Him. If you will keep your faith "strong through many trials," He will make something beautiful from the ashes (Isaiah 61:3). And on the day Jesus comes, you will receive "much praise and glory and honor."

Lord, You provide all the answers and direction I need. Keep me strong in the face of hardship.

AUGUST 22

THE LORD IS WITH YOU

I will fear no evil; for You are with me. . . . Surely goodness and mercy shall follow me all the days of my life.

PSALM 23:4, 6

The Lord, your Shepherd, is always with you. Just pause here for a moment and think about this beautiful truth: *the Lord God is with you every moment of every day.*

He stands steadfastly by your side in both sunshine and storms. He rejoices with you in the mountaintop moments and gently leads you through the valleys with the light of His love. He is your Fortress, your Shield, your Comforter, and your Guide.

In this world it's easy to be overwhelmed—by the headlines, by the troubles, by the worries big and small. But because you are God's own beloved child, you are never left to face this life on your own. The Lord God is with you, and surely His goodness and mercy shall follow you all the days of your life.

Lord, open my eyes to see the ways You work in my life. I'll follow You forever.

AUGUST 23

HIS BLESSINGS TO ENJOY

[I pray] that you may know what is the hope of His calling, what are the riches of the glory of His inheritance in the saints, and what is the exceeding greatness of His power toward us who believe.

EPHESIANS 1:18–19

Far too many Christians today are reluctant to truly savor God's blessings, to allow those blessings to fill them with joy and put smiles on their faces. But God did not intend for His people to be dour and sour!

Just look at the words used in Ephesians 1:18–19: *hope, riches, glory, inheritance, exceeding greatness.* These are actively joyful words. Today we have access to the power of God—the same power that the disciples witnessed and the same power that raised Jesus from the grave. And for our future, we have the promise of the unimaginable riches of our heavenly inheritance. With such blessings promised to us, how could we not smile and enjoy?

Lord, teach my heart to smile with joy at the abundance of Your blessings.

AUGUST 24

WE CAN DO ALL THINGS

I can do all things through Christ who strengthens me.

PHILIPPIANS 4:13

Philippians 4:13 is perhaps one of the most misused verses in the Bible. We see it applied to everything from careers to monetary success to selfish goals of every kind. But when the apostle Paul declared he could do all things through Christ, he didn't mean he could do whatever he wanted; Paul meant he could do whatever *He* wanted.

When we read Paul's words in context, we see he was actually talking about contentment. "I have learned in whatever state I am, to be content," he said (v. 11). Whether he was hungry or fed, abounding or in need, God enabled him to be content. He understood that God would supply all his needs (v. 19). Yes, we can do all things through Christ as we live according to His will.

Lord, help me walk in Your will and experience Your strength, confidence, and provision.

AUGUST 25

KNOWN BY NAME

"You have found grace in My sight, and I know you by name."

EXODUS 33:17

How do you feel when someone remembers your name? Now, how do you feel when someone, whom you've met several times, *doesn't* know your name?

To be known by our names establishes a connection. It says we're worth the trouble of remembering. If being known by our names by people here on earth is so significant, how much greater is it to be known by name by our Lord God? Is there anything more comforting than the knowledge that God knows each of us personally?

Our God is so powerful, so immense that He not only created all the stars and set them in their places in the heavens, but He also calls each by its name (Psalm 147:4). And He is so intensely personal that He knows *our names* and calls us to Him.

Lord, You are Creator of stars, Maker of mountains, Sculptor of seas . . . and yet You know my name! How wonderful You are!

AUGUST 26

WE CAN RELY ON HIS POWER

I will rather boast in my infirmities, that the power of Christ may rest upon me.

2 CORINTHIANS 12:9

Paul's life before he encountered Christ on the road to Damascus was one of religious fervor—but it was directed against believers in Jesus. He even worked to persecute "followers of the Way, hounding some to death, arresting both men and women" (Acts 22:4 NLT). But then he heard the voice of the Messiah, announcing, "I am Jesus the Nazarene," and he was never the same (v. 8 NLT).

Paul then told anyone who would listen all about the saving grace of Jesus. He was a changed man, but he was plagued by a "thorn in the flesh" (2 Corinthians 12:7). Though he begged God to remove it, God said, "My grace is all you need. My power works best in weakness" (v. 9 NLT). God's power promises to be greatest when it is all we have to rely on.

Lord, give me a humble spirit that fully relies on You.

AUGUST 27

HIS LOVE IS ENDLESS

By this we know love, because He laid down His life for us. And we also ought to lay down our lives for the brethren.

1 JOHN 3:16

Jesus Christ loves each of us with a love that has no end; it is full and complete and perfect.

His love is unconditional; you can't earn it, work for it, be good enough to have it, or convince God that you deserve it. No matter how great your sacrifice, it can never compare to the sacrifice Christ made for you. No matter how many good and wonderful things you do in this world, they will never match the good and wonderful work of Christ's gift of salvation. Because He was willing to give His life that you might have everlasting life, nothing is more important than the life of Christ within you.

And while you can't earn His gift of love, you can share it. Let His love flow through you to those around you.

Lord Jesus, You gave up heaven to die on a cross . . . for me. Help me love others with that same kind of sacrificial love.

GOD ANSWERS PRAYER

"Anyone who believes in me will do the same works I have done, and even greater works. . . . Ask me for anything in my name, and I will do it!"

JOHN 14:12, 14 NLT

As Jesus prepared to leave His disciples, He declared His followers would perform even greater wonders than He had. How was that possible? Perhaps one reason was that Jesus would be in heaven with the Father, interceding for His disciples. With that kind of support, nothing would be impossible for them!

But Jesus didn't stop there. He also told His disciples that whatever they asked in His name, He would do for them—and for us. That doesn't mean simply tacking His name onto the end of our prayers. It is praying in line with the will of the One whose name we use. Those prayers He will always answer.

Lord, may my prayers always line up with Your perfect will.

AUGUST 29

CALM FOR OUR ANGER

"I am slow to anger and filled with unfailing love and faithfulness."

EXODUS 34:6 NLT

There is righteous anger—that fury we feel about things we know God disapproves of. But too often our anger is far less noble. We feel angry, for instance, when we don't get our way, the day isn't unfolding according to our timetable, people let us down, or . . . the list goes on.

God knew much in this world would irritate us, so He calls us to be "slow to get angry" (James 1:19 NLT). We must not let rage be our master, prompting us to say or do things we will later regret. Anger can fuel foolishness and even harm relationships, but with God's help we can corral our emotions before any damage is done.

Turn to God. Let Him guide your words and actions. He will calm your spirit and give you His peace. Be slow to get angry with others, because God is slow to get angry with you.

Lord, when anger grabs hold of me,
help me to grab hold of You.

AUGUST 30

GOD'S PRODUCTIVE WORD

"My word . . . that goes forth from My mouth; it shall not return to Me void, but it shall accomplish what I please."

ISAIAH 55:11

Rain and snow will always fall. They will do what they are intended to do: water the earth and make the flowers and grains flourish. And just like "the rain [that] comes down, and the snow from heaven" (v. 10), the influence of God's Word cannot be halted. It will never fail to achieve its purpose.

Jesus commanded us to share the Word: "Go therefore and make disciples of all the nations" (Matthew 28:19), knowing that some would accept it eagerly, while others would reject it outright. Still others would hold it within themselves, pondering until the time was right. When we share the Word of God, we may not always see its work with our own eyes. But God has promised: His Word will accomplish what He sends it to do.

Lord, please give me the courage to share Your Word and the faith to know it is accomplishing Your will.

AUGUST 31

JESUS IS OUR EXAMPLE

"If I then, your Lord and Teacher, have washed your feet, you also ought to wash one another's feet."

JOHN 13:14

The Son of God Himself stooped to wash away the dust and grime of His disciples' feet. Yes, those same feet that He knew would in just a few hours run away from Him as fast as they could go. If Jesus would do that, what reason could we possibly give for not stooping to serve one another?

It's a lesson we still need today. Would we, like Jesus, stoop to serve anyone, much less people we knew were about to abandon us? We must not think too highly of ourselves (Romans 12:3), and we certainly must not consider ourselves too dignified to do anything that the One who stoops to save us did. We must humble ourselves to serve because Jesus humbled Himself to save.

Lord Jesus, You came to humbly serve Your people. Help me to do the same.

SEPTEMBER

SEPTEMBER 1

UNSHAKEN

He only is my rock and my salvation; He is my defense; I shall not be moved.

PSALM 62:6

As David wrote this psalm, he'd had just about everything thrown at him that the world could throw. He'd been lied to and about, betrayed, even attacked.

Sound familiar? Have you ever felt like a target for the world's arrows? We all have at one time or another, but listen to this amazing news: no matter how big the bomb, no matter how powerful our attackers, no matter how strong the storm, our God is bigger, more powerful, and stronger than any who would seek to stand against one of His beloved children.

He is our sure Foundation, our Defense, our Refuge to hide within. When we trust Him and His perfect care, the God who is great enough to raise Jesus from the tomb and save us from our sins will not let us be "shaken or discouraged" (AMP) or "moved."

Because of Your power, Lord, I trust You to take care of me.

SEPTEMBER 2

WISDOM GIVES LIFE

My son, give attention to my words. . . . For they are life to those who find them, and health to all their flesh.

PROVERBS 4:20, 22

Solomon knew that wisdom is both life and health to the one who hears and applies it. But applying the words of wisdom is not a onetime, quick-and-easy, no-thought-required kind of thing. It necessitates a dedication of heart, words, thoughts, and actions.

Wisdom lets no lie pass our lips. It keeps us focused on God's path, not distracted by the temptations of the world. And it keeps our feet moving ever closer to God, not turning aside to evil (vv. 23–27). Wisdom guards our very hearts, the wellsprings of all we do. It protects us, body and soul, from the ravages of sin and leads us to a life in God.

Lord, help me hide Your Word and Your wisdom in my heart, that I might not sin against You.

SEPTEMBER 3

CHRIST FULFILLS THE LAW

"Till heaven and earth pass away, one jot or one tittle will by no means pass from the law till all is fulfilled."

MATTHEW 5:18

Jesus spoke these words in Matthew as a defense against those who said He broke the law. He was accused of such things as blasphemy for forgiving a paralyzed man's sins (9:2–3), for eating with tax collectors and sinners (9:11), and for healing on the Sabbath (12:10–14). But Jesus assured His followers that He did not come "to destroy the Law or the Prophets. . . . but to fulfill" them (5:17). Not "one jot or one tittle"—not one smallest letter or detail—would pass away until it was all fulfilled.

The beauty of His promise is that we aren't held accountable for obeying every jot and tittle. Jesus Himself fulfilled all the prophecies and obeyed every law—down to the last letter. In doing so He set us free from the law and ushered in a new covenant built upon His love and grace.

Lord, I praise You for Your grace that frees me from a law I could never perfectly keep.

SEPTEMBER 4

DISCIPLINE BRINGS BLESSINGS

[Discipline] yields the peaceable fruit of righteousness to those who have been trained by it.

HEBREWS 12:11

No one likes to be disciplined, particularly adults. It just never feels good and rarely puts a smile on our faces or a spring in our steps. But when we choose to cooperate with God as He corrects us, blessings always come. Our eyes and hearts are opened not only to His ways but also to His amazing mercy and grace toward us when we stumble. And when we allow ourselves to be shaped and trained by His discipline, we are blessed with the opportunity for a closer walk with Him.

God is always working in and through His children, and His Spirit enables us to do worthwhile things for the kingdom. When we obey God and do His will and please Him, we can truly do all things through Christ whose Spirit dwells within us—and live a life of righteousness.

Father, thank You for loving me enough to correct me—and for the inevitable blessings that follow Your correction.

SEPTEMBER 5

AN OPEN INVITATION

Pray for all people. . . . [This] pleases God our Savior, who wants everyone to be saved.

1 TIMOTHY 2:1, 3–4 NLT

The Lord desires to save everyone. How do we know this? Because from the moment humankind sinned—even before—He had a plan to save us (1 Peter 1:20–21). Because He did nothing less than send His own Son to redeem us. And because He makes it easy for us to obtain salvation (Romans 10:9).

For this reason, we should "pray for all people"—from the neighbor next door to the one across town to the ruler in his palace. We should pray that their hearts would open to God—that they would hear His message and believe Jesus is the only way to God (John 14:6). God's invitation is open to everyone; no one is excluded.

Father, I pray that the hearts of all people would be touched by Your Word. I especially pray for . . .

SEPTEMBER 6

HIS STRENGTH

[I pray] that He would grant you, according to the riches of His glory, to be strengthened with might through His Spirit in the inner man, that Christ may dwell in your hearts through faith.

EPHESIANS 3:16–17

Strength is something we need a lot of these days. Not the superhero strength of a cartoon character or the muscled might of a bodybuilder, but the strength to get up each morning, to determinedly set our feet upon the floor, and to declare, "This day, I will serve the Lord. Whatever comes, I will follow Him."

But the beautiful thing about this strength we need is that it isn't our own. We don't have to rely on our own willpower, our own courage, our own steadfastness. God gives us this promise: we will be "strengthened . . . through *His* Spirit" (emphasis added). *His* will, *His* courage, *His* steadfastness—*His* strength. And even more wonderful than that is the fact that the Source of this power lives in our hearts.

Lord, strengthen me through Your Spirit within me so I may bring glory to Your name.

SEPTEMBER 7

PROMISES FULFILLED

The promise that he would be the heir of the world was not to Abraham or to his seed through the law, but through the righteousness of faith.

ROMANS 4:13

It was his faith that caused Abraham to be credited with righteousness, not keeping every last letter of the law. Likewise we are saved by faith, not by rule-keeping. And what is faith? Faith is believing when the odds are stacked against us (a nation born from a childless man?), following when we don't know where we're going (Go "to a land that I will show you," Genesis 12:1), and trusting God to do even the impossible (a son for a one-hundred-year-old man?).

But perhaps just as important as what faith is, is what faith is not. Faith is *not* perfection: "For we all stumble in many things" (James 3:2). Only Christ can claim the title of perfection. But our God is so generous, so loving, that He takes the perfection of Christ and shares it with all who are His own.

Lord, by faith I claim Your promises. And by faith, I trust You to save me.

SEPTEMBER 8

GOD THE SAVIOR

I will call upon the Lord, who is worthy to be praised; so shall I be saved from my enemies.

PSALM 18:3

David described God as a place and person of refuge, deliverance, safety. Whenever he needed rescue, David knew whom to turn to. What about you? When you need rescue, who do you go to first? Is it the Lord? Friends are marvelous, family is fabulous, preachers and teachers are excellent, but they are all wonderfully and imperfectly human. Only the Lord—only His guidance and wisdom—is perfect.

And ours is no timid, shrinking God. He is the Lord God Almighty, Creator of all and Ruler of all. When we have troubles, when we need help, when we need someone to get us through a frightening situation, *this* is whom to turn to! Perhaps just as amazing as the power and might of our Lord is the promise that when we do call out to Him, He comes to save us!

Lord, I praise You for always answering when I call.

SEPTEMBER 9

COMFORT TO THE ILL

"I, yes I, am the one who comforts you."

ISAIAH 51:12 NLT

The recognition of God's power to heal you and your loved ones is key to experiencing His tender love. Consider what James wrote: "The prayer of faith will save the sick, and the Lord will raise him up" (5:15). In this world, there is no such thing as a life without sickness and pain, without tears and sorrow. And while that truth may seem harsh and even discouraging, we also have this promise: God is with us, in sickness and health, until the day we join Him forever in heaven. As "the source of all comfort" (2 Corinthians 1:3 NLT), He ministers to us, holding us up with His own hand (Isaiah 41:10).

As we are comforted, we are also equipped—equipped to be a comfort to those we love when they need us (2 Corinthians 1:3–4). Then we spread the tender love and mercies of our Lord.

Thank You, Lord, for Your healing hand and Your comforting touch. Help me comfort others in turn.

SEPTEMBER 10

REJOICING WHILE WE WAIT

Our soul waits for the LORD; He is our help and our shield. For our heart shall rejoice in Him, because we have trusted in His holy name.

PSALM 33:20–21

W*aiting* and *rejoicing* aren't two words that we usually put together. But God does.

For us, *waiting* conjures up images of long lines and grouchy people. Or perhaps we think of unpaid bills and hospital rooms, worry and fear. But look at the key words in today's verses from Psalm 33: *help*, *shield*, *trust*, and yes, *rejoice*.

God never leaves us alone in our times of waiting. Our Lord is actively involved in every moment of our lives. In the times of waiting, He is working, helping, and shielding us. And when we trust in Him, He fills even our times of waiting with reasons to rejoice. We serve a great and mighty and endlessly loving God, who makes the impossible *possible* for those who believe.

Father, thank You for the comfort of knowing I never wait alone. Please open my heart to all my reasons to rejoice.

SEPTEMBER 11

HIS GREAT REWARD

Do not cast away your confidence, which has great reward. For you have need of endurance, so that after you have done the will of God, you may receive the promise.

HEBREWS 10:35–36

The original readers of this passage had endured insult, persecution, and even prison. And if they themselves hadn't experienced such, they had watched as those they cared about had. They had been able to endure so much because they trusted God would keep His promise. But in the face of still more troubles, their faith began to waver. It was because of this that the writer of Hebrews urged them to persevere, to be confident—to stay strong in the face of such opposition.

The same thing happens to us too, doesn't it? We endure, struggle, persevere. But at some point, we waver. That is not the time to give up; it's the time to turn to God, to His strength and renewal. Be confident. Trust God to keep His promises—and you will be blessed with His "great reward."

Lord, when my faith is wavering, remind me who You are—a God who keeps His promises.

SEPTEMBER 12

AN EVERLASTING LOVE

"Yes, I have loved you with an everlasting love."

JEREMIAH 31:3

You can't do it. There are lots of things you can do, but there are at least two things you can absolutely never, ever do.

The first is this: you can't convince God to stop loving you. You can't mess up enough, rebel enough, sin enough to change God's love for you. It is everlasting and eternal.

You also can't get yourself to heaven. But that's where God's everlasting love comes in. He knows you can't be perfect enough to be in His presence—not on your own. That's why He sent Jesus. He took our sins upon Himself and opened the pathway to heaven for those who choose to follow Him. All because God loves us with an everlasting love.

To know that I am so loved by the One who created everything is just astounding to me. I am overwhelmed by all You do for me. Thank You, my Lord, thank You.

SEPTEMBER 13

OUT OF REACH

He will hide me in his sanctuary. He will place me out of reach on a high rock. Then I will hold my head high above my enemies who surround me.

PSALM 27:5–6 NLT

Whether it's the office bully, that grown-up mean girl who has yet to learn the meaning of kindness, or the snares of the devil himself, the fact is that we have enemies in this world. They chip, chip, chip away at us, day by day. Some seek to intimidate, others to raise themselves up by pulling us down. But some—like the devil—seek our destruction. They don't know the power of our God.

The Lord is our light and salvation—so why should we be afraid (v. 1)? He promises us His strength and His courage, and He places us high upon a rock. Yes, the enemies will still hurl their barbs and arrows, but we will be safely out of reach, hidden in the sanctuary of God.

Lord, from the safety of Your sanctuary, I will shout with joy and sing Your praises.

SEPTEMBER 14

A GODLY LIFE

By his divine power, God has given us everything we need for living a godly life. . . . He has given us great and precious promises.

2 PETER 1:3–4 NLT

Do you ever feel as though you just don't have what it takes to be holy, as God is holy? The apostle Peter insists otherwise. God's "divine power . . . has given us everything we need for a godly life." We have His Word, which contains the complete message of salvation. As believers we have His Spirit, who reveals the truth of God's Word to us. And we have all of God's guarantees—His "great and precious promises."

These promises help us in our life here on earth. And there are also the promises that enable us to have eternal life—promises for forgiveness and mercy and grace. Through these promises of God, we "share his divine nature" (v. 4 NLT) as we are molded and shaped into the image of our Lord. Holiness is within our reach!

Lord, thank You for giving me everything I need to live a faithful life—Your Word, Your Spirit, Your promises.

SEPTEMBER 15

AN INNER COMPASS

"I will send you the Advocate—the Spirit of truth. He will come to you from the Father and will testify all about me."

JOHN 15:26 NLT

Who—or what—is your guide for life? To whom do you turn for daily guidance on how to live life, what to do, where to go, whom to see, how to make decisions? Is it the stock market, your career path, or family expectations? The Scriptures say the only Guide worth trusting is the Holy Spirit. Because He is the only One who knows your past completely, from the moment you were conceived to the present, and He knows your future from this day to eternity. Only He knows God's plan and purpose for you, what is fully good and right for you.

The Spirit of truth is the inner compass for your life, pointing you toward what Jesus would be, say, or do. God desires to make His will known to you, and He gives you this knowledge through the indwelling of the Holy Spirit. Trust Him to be your daily Guide.

Lord, by Your Spirit, lead me to Christlike living.

SEPTEMBER 16

CONSTANT FELLOWSHIP

He is the one who is eternal life. He was with the Father, and then he was revealed to us. . . . Our fellowship is with the Father and with his Son, Jesus Christ.

1 JOHN 1:2–3 NLT

Jesus has been with God since the beginning . . . and an eternity before that: "In the beginning was the Word, and the Word was with God, and the Word was God" (John 1:1). Even when Jesus came to live among us on earth, He lived in full fellowship with His Father—until the cross.

Everything changed at the cross. Jesus took all our sins upon Himself and God had to turn away. There was a separation that had never been before, a separation between God the Father and God the Son, so there could be a union between us and God that had never been before. Now we too can dwell in the constant care and presence of God in full fellowship with Him. What a privilege, what a promise, what a Savior!

Lord Jesus, You have always been with the Father—and I praise You for giving me a way to always be with the Father too.

SEPTEMBER 17

ALL WHO BELIEVE

All who believe in him are made right with God. . . . Faith comes from hearing, that is, hearing the Good News about Christ.

ROMANS 10:4, 17 NLT

God's Word tells us clearly how to become His children; it is not some secret we have to decode or unlock (v. 9). It is right there in His Word, for all the world—for us—to see.

When we truly listen to and meditate upon His Word, we find that it is, in fact, *truth*. Recognizing that God's Word is truth, we then can't help but believe. And as we learn more and dig deeper, we discover that greatest of truths—that Jesus really is the Son of God, that He died to save us from our sins, and that by choosing to follow Him, we can one day join Him in heaven. Believing that Jesus is who He says He is leads to faith, which leads to obedience and salvation. And then we can lay claim to all the promises He offers—strength and peace for this day and a home in heaven for eternity.

Lord, place within my heart a hunger to know more and more about You.

SEPTEMBER 18

NONE SO GREAT AS GOD

There is no one like the God of Jeshurun, who rides the heavens to help you, and in His excellency on the clouds. The eternal God is your refuge, and underneath are the everlasting arms.

DEUTERONOMY 33:26–27

The next time you are in need of rescue, remember the imagery of this passage from Deuteronomy: the Lord God of Israel riding on the clouds of the heavens, in all His might and majesty, charging forth to defend and rescue you.

Our God is not meek or timid; He is not passively watching the events of this world unfold from His throne room in heaven. He does not sit idly by while His children are attacked. Our God is a Red Sea–parting, walls of Jericho–tumbling, halt-the-sun-in-the-sky God who storms down from the skies to protect, defend, and rescue those who love Him.

This God, who is infinitely strong and mighty, is the same God who gently and lovingly tucks His children into the protection of His everlasting arms. There is none so great as our God.

Father, I'm so grateful to serve a God of power and might, who is willing to rescue and shelter me.

SEPTEMBER 19

YOU CAN ENDURE

Count it all joy when you fall into various trials, knowing that the testing of your faith produces patience.

JAMES 1:2–3

Patience has been defined as learning to accept difficult situations without giving God a deadline for their removal. We know we need patience, but we generally shun the process by which we learn it. We want it now! So because we cannot wait for God's direction, we all too often move ahead on our own initiative—with all too predictable, disastrous results.

The Old Testament admonishes us: "Wait on the Lord; be of good courage, and He shall strengthen your heart; wait, I say, on the Lord!" (Psalm 27:14). The Bible promises that trials and tribulations will produce patience as you learn to bear up, to persevere, and to keep holding on, even when there is no worldly help in sight. If you do so, God will grant you all the endurance you need.

Lord, help me to persevere through the hard times for Your glory. Grant me patience as I wait on Your deliverance.

SEPTEMBER 20

IN THE MORNING

Weeping may endure for a night, but joy comes in the morning.

PSALM 30:5

During our lives, we will all face difficult days. We will face enemies within and without. We will make mistakes that cause us pain and sorrow. But whatever comes—whether from our own sins, the attacks of others, or the whims of a fallen world—we must remember God *and* we must sing His praises.

There will be times when our words and actions hurt others, and times others' words and actions hurt us. Tears will fall, and hearts will break. And the things of this world will prove utterly unreliable. *But* . . . the Lord our God will not abandon us. His love and favor will never leave us. He will not allow us to be snatched away. We sing our praises to God, because He will give us joy in the morning.

Father, I praise You for Your great love that showers me with mercy and grace and joy.

SEPTEMBER 21

JESUS IS COMING

"They will see the Son of Man coming in the clouds with great power and glory."

MARK 13:26

The day will come when "heaven and earth will pass away" because they are temporary things, not eternal (v. 31). But the words of Christ are eternal; they will never fade or pass away. Every prediction He has spoken will happen, just as He has said. And He has said the day is coming when He will return and claim His own. That will be a day of unimaginable joy for His children.

Only the Father knows when that day will be (v. 32). But He will come, and it will be like "a thief in the night" (1 Thessalonians 5:2). Therefore we must be ready. We must surrender our lives to Him, letting His love permeate our every thought, word, and action, and relying fully on His grace. For He has promised, and He is coming.

Lord, You know the day and the hour of Jesus' return. Help me to be steadfast and faithful as I wait to see Jesus face-to-face.

SEPTEMBER 22

THE ANGELS REJOICE

"There is joy in the presence of the angels of God over one sinner who repents."

LUKE 15:10

Luke 15 tells three parables, each a tender reflection of the Father's love for those who are lost. There is the lost sheep—not left to wander alone, but sought for and carried back to the flock. There is the lost coin—not given up on, but carefully searched for until found. And there is the lost son—the one the father never stopped watching for, the one the father embraced when he at last came home.

Notice, though, what happens at the end of each parable—not scolding, punishment, or public shame—but rejoicing! In the first two parables, the angels of heaven joined in the joyous celebration. No matter your past, your mistakes, your sins, when you go to God, don't hang your head in shame. Know this: you were sought for, welcomed, and wanted. You are found—and all the angels rejoice!

Lord, thank You for welcoming me to my home by Your side.

SEPTEMBER 23

THE LORD RESCUES US

I entrust my spirit into your hand. Rescue me,
Lord, for you are a faithful God.

PSALM 31:5 NLT

Growth in our relationship with the Lord begins with this statement: "I entrust my spirit into your hand." Until we surrender and invite Him, as the Lord and Master of our hearts, our thoughts, our souls, and our lives, to take over, we will struggle to fix things on our own.

When we entrust our whole being to the Lord, He rescues and redeems us—from sin and from death, but also from the evils of this life. He becomes our firm foundation and our hiding place. He guides and leads us in the way we should go. He foils the traps of our enemies and gives us the strength to withstand their attacks (v. 8). Why does He do this? "[He cares] about the anguish of my soul" (v. 7 NLT). When we commit our spirits to His keeping, the Lord rescues us.

Lord, thank You for being my Rescuer and Redeemer.

SEPTEMBER 24

UNFAILING LOVE

Your unfailing love is better than life itself; how I praise you!

PSALM 63:3 NLT

Psalm 63 is one of the most beautifully moving expressions of trust and praise. It is David's psalm as he fled to the wilderness. Even in his troubled state, with enemies close at hand, David not only sought the Lord but praised Him: "I will lift up my hands in Your name" (v. 4). He trusted the Lord to save Him: "Your right hand upholds me" (v. 8). But perhaps most remarkable, David sang of the unfailing love of His God.

The Lord reaches down and loves, heals, strengthens, and saves us. Because we are His, that always faithful love is ours. We should spend our entire lives telling the world of His greatness and telling the Lord how much we love Him. Like David, let's bless Him while we live.

Lord, I lift up my hands in praise to You for Your lovingkindness.

SEPTEMBER 25

GOD SATISFIES

Oh, that men would give thanks to the LORD for His goodness. . . . For He satisfies the longing soul, and fills the hungry soul with goodness.

PSALM 107:8–9

That longing for home, for peace, for rest—all those things live deep within our hearts because God put them there. Why? So we will seek Him, because ultimately He is the only One who can satisfy. He is the forever home our souls seek (John 14:23); He is peace beyond understanding (Philippians 4:7); He is rest when we are weary (Matthew 11:28).

As the Israelites journeyed through the wilderness, God satisfied their thirst with water from rock and their hunger with manna from heaven. "He delivered them out of their distresses. And He led them forth by the right way" (Psalm 107:6–7), because they were His children. God will do the same for us—He will satisfy our deepest longings for Him, because we are His.

Lord, quench my thirst for You.

SEPTEMBER 26

GIFT OF ACCOUNTABILITY

Two are better than one, because they have a good reward for their labor. For if they fall, one will lift up his companion.

ECCLESIASTES 4:9–10

The idea of being accountable to someone for our actions in life can feel like sandpaper rubbing against the rough edges of our egos and pride. But believe it or not, accountability is actually a promised gift. God never calls any of His children to go it alone in their walk with Him. We need each other not only for help and encouragement, but also for accountability and to be effective witnesses to those God brings into our lives.

When we are honest with God and a trusted, godly friend, the commitment we have to a deeper walk with our Savior becomes a spiritual bond that will not be broken. Through another's eyes we see ourselves, our actions, our motives more clearly—accountability saves us from our blind spots.

Lord, thank You for providing a way to see my hidden faults—through the eyes of an accountability partner and friend.

SEPTEMBER 27

HEALING FOR THE HEART

He heals the brokenhearted and bandages their wounds.

PSALM 147:3 NLT

Sometimes in life, for various reasons, relationships fall apart. At that point, every emotion imaginable enters your life, leaving you hurt, broken, confused, and wondering how in the world this could have happened.

When your heart is broken, know that God stands ready to give you His guidance. Ask Him, and He will show you the way to go—but you must ask in faith, believing He will answer, and then be willing to listen carefully to His voice. He will guide you when you are truly ready to follow. And each step along the way, He will give you His strength and comfort, holding you close to His own heart (Isaiah 40:11). Depend on the One who loves you with an everlasting love. He is the perfect Healer for your broken heart.

Lord Jesus, You know all about the pain in my heart. Please heal me and show me the way to go forward.

SEPTEMBER 28

IF YOU RETURN

The Lord your God is gracious and merciful, and will not turn His face from you if you return to Him.

2 CHRONICLES 30:9

It had been too long since God's people had been faithful to Him, but King Hezekiah was determined to turn the people back to the Lord. So he invited all of Israel and Judah to Jerusalem to celebrate the Passover Feast. Many were "stiff-necked" (v. 8) and refused to return. But others did return—to Jerusalem and to the Lord—and He did not turn His face from them.

We all have our moments when we wander away from the Lord. When we realize our wrongs, we may long to return to Him but fear His reaction. *Will God still forgive?* If this is you, claim this promise from 2 Chronicles as your own: "The Lord your God is gracious and merciful, and will not turn His face from you if you return to Him."

Lord, forgive me for the times I turn away from You. I'm so grateful for Your mercy—and so thankful You never turn from me.

SEPTEMBER 29

A SPIRIT OF POWER

God has not given us a spirit of fear, but of power and of love and of a sound mind.

2 TIMOTHY 1:7

Paul's words to Timothy are just as reassuring to us as they were to him all those years ago. They remind us of who our God is and who we are in Him—something all too easy to forget in this world in which we're so often afraid. The day-to-day conflicts of life, the grown-up bullies and intimidators—not to mention the daily headlines—can leave us feeling anything but brave and powerful, anything but loving.

That's when we must draw upon the Spirit of God who lives within us, allowing Him to remind us of who He is and who we can be when we rely upon His power. Through Him, we *can* face every situation without fear or helplessness. God has provided all we need in His Spirit.

Father, when fears threaten to overwhelm me, remind me of who You are—and the strength I have in You.

SEPTEMBER 30

REAP A HARVEST

The fruit of righteousness is sown in peace by those who make peace.

JAMES 3:18

Facetious, derisive, demeaning remarks: these are the things of sitcoms and put-downs. The world laughs at them and at those to whom they are directed. But God does not.

Stubborn, aggressive, determined to have our own way, willing to cut corners or step on others to lift ourselves up—that's the way to succeed, business says. But God does not. Selfish, self-seeking, self-promoting—that's the way to get what you deserve, society says. But God does not.

Instead, God offers this wisdom: be pure, love peace, be gentle, be thoughtful, be willing to yield, show mercy, do good to all, and be sincere (v. 17). These are the seeds of peace. And when we sow them, God promises to reap in us a harvest of righteousness.

Lord, when those around me sow seeds of discord, help me sow seeds of peace instead.

OCTOBER

OCTOBER 1

STRONG CHARACTER

We can rejoice, too, when we run into problems and trials, for we know that they help us develop endurance. And endurance develops strength of character.

ROMANS 5:3–4 NLT

A person's character is demonstrated by the way he or she reacts to hardship, trials, and unpleasant circumstances. God will use ordeals, difficulties, and adversities to mature us into people who look like His Son. No one enjoys problems or trials, but by faith—and sometimes with the gift of hindsight—we can begin to understand how God may use them to strengthen our faith.

When you think of your life with God, think of the way He wraps you in His loving care. Through your obedience, His grace washes over your life like sunlight on a cloudless day and deepens your godly character. Nothing can separate you from the presence of God as you walk hand in hand with Him.

Lord, when I face hard times, help me see the ways You use my difficult days to shape my character.

OCTOBER 2

CROWNED WITH KINDNESS

Bless the L*ORD*, *. . . who crowns you with lovingkindness and tender mercies.*

PSALM 103:1, 4

Forgiven, healed, and redeemed. These are the benefits God promises to His children. Why does such a good and perfect God choose to so richly bless such a sinful and imperfect people? Why does He offer royal crowns to common folk? The answer is as beautiful as its benefits: because of His "lovingkindness and tender mercies."

Psalm 103 lists many of the "benefits" God bestows on us, including renewed strength, righteousness, and justice (vv. 2, 5–6). God loves each of us perfectly and generously. When we respond to this lavish love—when we love, seek, and praise Him—He blesses us. We are forgiven, healed, and redeemed, because ours is a God of "lovingkindness and tender mercies."

Lord, may I never forget Your love, mercy, and grace. Help me love You with all that I am.

OCTOBER 3

THE LORD WILL KEEP YOU

My help comes from the Lord, who made heaven and earth. . . . He who keeps you will not slumber.

PSALM 121:2–3

Sleep is supposed to just happen. We lie down, close our eyes . . . and sleep. Too often, though, our thoughts spin around like the wheels of a runaway train. *What-ifs*, *what-shoulds*, and *if-onlys* haunt us and rob us of our rest.

But the old adage is true: *Cast your cares upon the Lord* (1 Peter 5:7)—*He's going to be up all night anyway.*

You see, God gives us a promise: He will never sleep, never slumber, never take a day—or night—off. He is always aware of what's happening in our lives. Always watching, always keeping, always working for our good. When anxious thoughts keep us from much-needed rest, we can pour out our hearts to Him. And He will give us rest (Matthew 11:28) . . . while He keeps watch all through the night.

Lord, I entrust all my worries and cares to You. Please fill me with Your peace and help me rest.

OCTOBER 4

GAIN CONTENTMENT

Godliness with contentment is great gain. For we brought nothing into this world, and it is certain we can carry nothing out.

1 TIMOTHY 6:6–7

Contentment is a gift only God can give. So many times our desire for material possessions overshadows our relationship with the Lord. We can cultivate contentment if we see God as our sole Provider and focus on the necessities of life. For while God will often supply our *wants* out of His goodness and grace, He has promised to supply all of our *needs* (Philippians 4:19).

Learn to express your gratitude for what you have. Your greatest source of contentment will be found when you "take delight in the Lord" (Psalm 37:4 NLT). Stop for a moment and take inventory of all God has blessed you with and give thanks for each of these things. As your list of blessings grows, so will your sense of contentment.

Lord, when I review the multitude of Your blessings, I am overwhelmed with gratitude. Thank You for Your faithfulness!

OCTOBER 5

CONFIDENCE IN PRAYER

If we ask anything according to His will, He hears us. And if we know that He hears us, whatever we ask, we know that we have the petitions that we have asked of Him.

1 JOHN 5:14–15

Powerful promises are packed into these verses from 1 John. First, God hears us. Yes, it's true that God already knows what we're going to say (Psalm 139:4). Isaiah even tells us that while we're "still talking," He will "go ahead and answer [our] prayers" (65:24 NLT). But don't discount the fact that God *listens.* Because sometimes isn't that what we need most? But of course God doesn't *just* listen.

If we ask anything that matches His will, God grants our "petitions." How do we know if our prayers are His will? We seek His truth in wise counsel, in prayer, and especially in His Word. As we study Scripture, He gently draws our hearts into line with His will. And we can then go before Him knowing He will grant what we seek.

Lord, thank You for listening to me. Please teach my heart to desire only the things that please You.

OCTOBER 6

EACH HAS A GIFT

God has given each of you a gift from his great variety of spiritual gifts. Use them well to serve one another.

1 PETER 4:10 NLT

It's easy to look at the gifts of others and then see ourselves as lacking. It's then far too tempting to permit ourselves to do nothing because we are not gifted in the same way. We may think our gift isn't quite up to par, or even that we have no gift at all. But God's Word clearly promises that "God has given each of [us] a gift."

With our gift comes a responsibility to use it. Not just for ourselves, but to "minister" to others. Some gifts are easy to see, such as the ability to preach, to sing, to lead. Others are quieter, such as the ability to encourage with a word, to comfort with a meal, or to gently hold the hand of one who is ill.

You have a gift—how will you use it?

Lord, please show me the gift You've given me—and how I can best use it to serve others and glorify You.

OCTOBER 7

A RICH RELATIONSHIP

"A person is a fool to store up earthly wealth but not have a rich relationship with God."

LUKE 12:21 NLT

So many times in life we get sidetracked by our grown-up toys and material possessions. True satisfaction in life flows not from stuff, but from fulfilling the purpose for which we were created: to enjoy an intimate relationship with God our Father.

Acquiring the latest and greatest, biggest and best as a substitute for a real relationship with God will ultimately leave our hearts feeling hollow and empty. Just as important, the example we set for our loved ones about the importance of a relationship with God influences the way they choose their priorities. God has promised that He has good plans for us (Jeremiah 29:11). Trust His wisdom. And for your own soul's sake, invest in a "rich relationship" with your heavenly Father.

Father, please turn my eyes and heart away from worldly riches and toward the riches of a relationship with You.

OCTOBER 8

POWER TO PLEASE

Don't look out only for your own interests, but take an interest in others, too. . . . God is working in you, giving you the desire and the power to do what pleases him.

PHILIPPIANS 2:4, 13 NLT

In today's culture, looking out for Number Two is not a popular approach to life. Personal desires and selfish ambitions are the driving force in the way many people think and live. But that kind of lifestyle is the direct opposite of what God desires for His people.

The Lord wants to live within and through you, so that—with every step, every decision, every conversation, every thought—you show the world His great love. Jesus came to serve (Matthew 20:28), and as you allow Him to work through you, you'll find your life becoming one of service too. It won't be a life of grudging servitude, but one where every experience becomes a beautiful blending of His perfection and your unique talents, traits, and personality.

Lord, please work through me, giving me the desire and the power to serve those around me.

OCTOBER 9

SPIRIT-FILLED INFLUENCE

"You will receive power when the Holy Spirit comes upon you. And you will be my witnesses, telling people about me everywhere . . . to the ends of the earth."

ACTS 1:8 NLT

Becoming a godly role model is a gift only God can give. Through His divine providence, certain people have been placed in your life, including friends, coworkers, neighbors, and relatives. Accept the blessing and the responsibility to be a faithful example and look forward to the adventure of impacting others with the love of God in your heart.

When you place your faith in Christ, His Spirit comes to live within you, to enable you to be your best self. Everything you need to be a powerful witness for the Lord is available to you. You need only ask and then surrender to His leading. God, through His gracious mercy, promises to deliver.

Lord, fill me with Your Spirit that I may be Your witness everywhere I go.

OCTOBER 10

FORGIVING HEALS US

Be kind to one another, tenderhearted, forgiving one another, even as God in Christ forgave you.

EPHESIANS 4:32

God has commanded us as His followers to forgive those who wrong us. He offers no conditions under which we can avoid this instruction.

That doesn't mean that forgiving is easy or even instantaneous. Neither does it mean that we were not wronged. Often forgiveness is a process: the bigger the wrong, the longer and more painful that process can be. Forgiving is taking our hurt and anger to God and begging Him to help us set it aside. It is choosing to pray for the person who wronged us. But most of all, forgiving is about us. While we pray blessings on the offender, it always heals us.

Lord, I give this hurt and anger to You. Help me forgive the person who hurt me and guide him/her ever closer to You.

OCTOBER 11

SHARE IN GLORY

Think about the things of heaven, not the things of earth. For you died to this life, and your real life is hidden with Christ in God.

COLOSSIANS 3:2–3 NLT

Colossians 3 tells us that, by choosing to follow Jesus, we have joined our lives with His, so we are to see the people, things, and events around us not as the world views them, but as God does. So while that friend's slight *feels* awfully important, will it matter in heaven? As we look at our lives, what are the things that matter to our Father?

When we view our lives through our Father's eyes, we learn what is of true importance and what we can lay aside as empty pursuits. If our greatest pursuit is to claim the promise that we will one day appear with Jesus in glory, we must keep our lives "hidden with Christ in God," submitting all to His will and ways.

Lord, show me my life through Your eyes, and please help me focus on the things that are important to You.

OCTOBER 12

SILENCE ACCUSERS

Submit yourselves to every ordinance of man for the Lord's sake. . . . For this is the will of God, that by doing good you may put to silence the ignorance of foolish men.

1 PETER 2:13, 15

Call it whatever you like—discrimination, bias, persecution—but the attitude against Christians in our society and world is often hostile. The followers of God have long endured such treatment; indeed, since Jesus came people have opposed Christians. There have always been those who are contentious to people of faith.

So what is a Christian to do? "Submit yourselves to every ordinance of man for the Lord's sake." We render unto Caesar that which belongs to Caesar (Matthew 22:21). Until the day that following the law means breaking God's law, we respectfully obey. We return goodness for hostility. And by doing so, we remove any opportunity for accusation.

Lord, please give me wisdom in dealing with this world. Help me show others who You really are.

OCTOBER 13

POURED INTO OUR HEARTS

Hope does not disappoint, because the love of God has been poured out in our hearts by the Holy Spirit who was given to us.

ROMANS 5:5

Hope, for a child of God, is not a starry-eyed optimism. Instead, it is a confident assurance, a certainty, a bold belief that our future home is a heavenly one. It is trusting in God's promises and waiting with joyful expectation for the day when He will keep them.

And all that confidence, certainty, and trust are based on one thing: the unending, unconditional, unlimited love of God. A love that He poured out at creation as He made us in His own image. A love that He poured out on the cross to wash away our sins. And a love that He poured right into our own hearts with the gift of His Holy Spirit.

With a love that great, our God will surely never disappoint our hope.

Father, You love me and will keep Your promises; therefore I will hope in You.

OCTOBER 14

ALIVE THROUGH CHRIST

Reckon yourselves to be dead indeed to sin, but alive to God in Christ Jesus our Lord.

ROMANS 6:11

When Jesus died on the cross, the penalty for our sins was nailed to that cross with Him. But sin itself—and the temptation to sin—is still very much alive.

The good news is that we are not left to combat it alone. The Holy Spirit of God lives within us to enable us to resist sin and to guide us toward God. But we must do our part too. We must cooperate with the Spirit by not presenting ourselves "as instruments of unrighteousness" (v. 13)—which is just a fancy way of saying we don't need to go looking for trouble. Or as Proverbs 6:18 says, we shouldn't have "feet that are swift in running to evil."

When we consider ourselves dead to sin—resisting it at every turn—that is when we become alive through Christ.

Lord, please use my life as an instrument to do what is good and right and glorifying to You.

OCTOBER 15

THE LIGHT OF THE LORD

Once you were full of darkness, but now you have light from the Lord. So live as people of light! For this light within you produces only what is good and right and true.

EPHESIANS 5:8–9 NLT

We were once "full of darkness" . . . before we knew Jesus. But then we accepted Jesus as our Lord and resolved to follow Him. He came into our lives blasting away the darkness within us and filling us with His light.

So, having been blessed with His light, should we then go back to the same ways of darkness? Of course not! We should "live as people of light." The Spirit who lives inside us will help us on our way. Then we'll not only live in the light of Jesus, we will also bear the fruit of that light—"what is good and right and true." We'll shine the way toward the Light of the world, King Jesus.

Yes, we were once in darkness, but now we walk in light.

Lord, I praise You for Your light that chases away my darkness. Let me be a beacon to others for You.

OCTOBER 16

THE ANSWER TO FEAR

Because you have made the Lord, who is my refuge, even the Most High, your dwelling place, no evil shall befall you.

PSALM 91:9–10

Psalm 91 offers God's people a beautiful picture of His all-powerful protection. It begins by proclaiming that, as His children, we dwell in "the secret place of the Most High" (v. 1). He covers us with His feathers, shelters us under His wings, and gives us His truth to be our shield (v. 4).

There may be terrors that stalk the night and arrows that fly in the day. There may be a pestilence in the darkness and a plague at the noontide (vv. 5–6). But we will have no reason to fear. Because we have made the Lord our dwelling place, "no evil shall befall" us.

God addresses every fear of our hearts and declares it is no match for His power and might. He is the answer to all our fears.

Lord, You know the things that frighten me, that make me doubt and tremble. Shelter me with Your all-powerful protection.

OCTOBER 17

WE WILL SEE HIS SALVATION

"He shall call upon Me, and I will answer him; I will be with him in trouble; I will deliver him and honor him. With long life I will satisfy him, and show him My salvation."

PSALM 91:15–16

The promises laid out in these verses are crucial ones. For believers, they form a foundation for faith and give us a reason to place our hope in the Lord. Because He has settled His love on us, we are enabled to settle our love on Him—remember, we love because He first loved us (Psalm 91:14; 1 John 4:19). To settle our love on Him means He is first in our lives; we put His perfect will before our own selfish wants and ambitions.

When we do this, the Lord gives us His beautiful and sustaining promises: He will answer when we call. He will be present with us in our troubles. He will rescue us from the enemies that ever threaten to overwhelm us. When we set our love on the Lord, He promises that we will see His salvation. We will see heaven. And we will see our Lord and King, face to glorious face.

Father, I settle my love on You, and I praise You for the love You settle on me.

OCTOBER 18

UNBREAKABLE COVENANT

"The mountains shall depart and the hills be removed, but My kindness shall not depart from you, nor shall My covenant of peace be removed."

ISAIAH 54:10

When Isaiah gave this prophecy, he foresaw the Israelites suffering in exile. God would allow this suffering because of Israel's sins, but the time of suffering would end. God would rescue His people because of the everlasting covenant He had made with them.

God also makes a covenant with us, through the death, burial, and resurrection of Christ. Though His covenant is offered to everyone, we enter into its promises only when we accept Jesus as our Savior and obey Him as our Lord. When we do that, we discover the never-ending faithfulness of our Lord as He promises, "In righteousness you shall be established; you shall be far from oppression, for you shall not fear; and from terror, for it shall not come near you" (v. 14).

Lord, I praise You for Your kindness and for Your everlasting covenant with me.

OCTOBER 19

NICE GUYS ALWAYS WIN

Put on your new nature, and be renewed as you learn to know your Creator and become like him. . . . You must clothe yourselves with tenderhearted mercy, kindness, humility, gentleness, and patience.

COLOSSIANS 3:10, 12 NLT

When God's children learn to depend on Him for wisdom, insight, and understanding, they always win. One of the key lessons of life is to recognize that without God, life will be a struggle that—in the end—no one wins. But with God all things are possible.

Many times we allow ambition to influence who we become and how we live. During those times money and power become the center of our attention, and we lose spiritually.

God will not settle for last place; He wants to be first in our hearts. In order to win spiritually, we must lose ourselves completely in the will of God. As we "put on [our] new nature," clothing ourselves with mercy and kindness, gentleness and patience in all situations, we will win both renewal and reward.

Lord, help me clothe myself with a new nature—one of kindness and humility, gentleness and love.

OCTOBER 20

JESUS OUR CORNERSTONE

"Behold, I lay in Zion a chief cornerstone, elect, precious, and he who believes on Him will by no means be put to shame."

1 PETER 2:6

Jesus is the Cornerstone of the new covenant and of the Christian's faith. He is the foundational stone upon which all else is built. He is utterly trustworthy and reliable. And those who faithfully follow Him will never be let down. Jesus will not fail.

But many will never accept Him. They will reject Him as nothing more than a good teacher or a wise man. Their rejection, however, does not change who He is as the Son of God, nor does it change the fact that He is the only way to salvation.

Those who accept Jesus as the Cornerstone of their faith are blessed. A life built on believing in Jesus and His promises "will by no means be put to shame."

Jesus, You are the One upon whom I can always depend. I will build my faith on You, my life on You.

OCTOBER 21

BLESSINGS FOR THOSE WHO TRUST

Trust in the Lord with all your heart; do not depend on your own understanding. Seek his will in all you do, and he will show you which path to take.

PROVERBS 3:5–6 NLT

No matter where you travel in life, or what challenges you may face, God goes before you, inviting you to "trust in the Lord with all your heart." When you hand your troubles and your troubled emotions over to Him, He will always be there. Depend on His Spirit to give you strength and to "show you which path to take" every day through whatever life may bring.

God's desire is that you will know intimately the loving grace and mercy only He can give. He will fill each day with the power of His presence as you trust in Him.

Father God, You are all-knowing and all-powerful. Thank You for the ways You guide me to do Your will.

OCTOBER 22

GOD BLESSES THE PATIENT

Be patient, brethren, until the coming of the Lord.

JAMES 5:7

We live in an instant world—instant information, instant technology, even instant soup. So patience is not a virtue we excel at.

Learning to wait on the Lord doesn't come naturally, but it is something we can all work on. Jesus is coming back. While that promise gives us such hope for the future, it also means we must wait, calmly and cheerfully, until He fulfills it.

That means persevering to the end—doing all the good and right things God has told us to do. Loving Him, loving others, serving, forgiving, helping, being kind and generous and compassionate. It means not grumbling against one another (v. 9). The Lord is coming, and He will bless for all eternity those who patiently wait for Him.

Lord, help me to wait patiently for You and to offer patience to everyone in my life.

OCTOBER 23

EVERY PROMISE KEPT

Joyful are those who have the God of Israel as their helper, whose hope is in the LORD their God. . . . He keeps every promise forever.

PSALM 146:5–6 NLT

When life with its twists and turns takes you down unexpected and difficult roads, it can sometimes feel strange to praise the Lord. Yet He seeks your praise in all things. Remember that God is good and always gives ample reason to praise Him.

God's overriding purpose for your life is to glorify Him, and He will use any means to accomplish that. As you open your heart to see your life's circumstances the way He does, praise Him who "keeps every promise forever." He will never leave you to sort out issues on your own. Those who rely on Him as their "helper" are "joyful," always finding reasons to praise.

Father, make me ever mindful of my purpose to glorify You in every circumstance. Fill me with Your joy as I await the fulfilling of all Your promises.

OCTOBER 24

SHARE IN CHRIST'S GLORIES

Exhort one another daily, while it is called "Today," lest any of you be hardened through the deceitfulness of sin. For we have become partakers of Christ if we hold the beginning of our confidence steadfast to the end.

HEBREWS 3:13–14

There are those who say they believe Jesus is the Son of God, but then later they deny Him and turn their backs on Him. It doesn't happen all that often, but it does happen.

The greater danger is not a sudden denial; rather it is from a gradual drifting away—a slipping into sin here, a sliding away from godly practice there. A little neglecting of the Bible, a little sleeping in on Sundays, a little forgetting to pray, until one day we wake up to find our hearts have hardened to Him.

As believers we must lift each other up, encouraging each other to stay close to God, and warning each other if someone seems to be slipping away. If we stay faithful, we will become "partakers" in the glories of Christ.

Lord, fill my life with believers who will love me enough to warn me when I am slipping away.

OCTOBER 25

LEARN GOD'S WAY

Teach me, O Lord, the way of Your statutes, and I shall keep it to the end. Give me understanding, and I shall keep Your law; indeed, I shall observe it with my whole heart.

PSALM 119:33–34

If you want to please God and honor Him with your life, you must get to know His Word. The Bible warns us of the challenges we may face, steers us toward the heart of God, and gives us the wisdom to flourish in every situation we face.

Many Christians have neglected God's Word, relying on others to simply tell them what it says. But they have missed the power and hope awaiting them there. As we study and absorb the Bible's truths for ourselves, we create storehouses of knowledge and wisdom that are always available to help us in tough times and to increase our joy in the good times. Let God's Word strengthen your Christian walk by learning "the way of [His] statutes."

Lord, help me read Your Word faithfully so I will be ready for any circumstance I face.

OCTOBER 26

GOD'S WORD IS COMPLETE

Stand fast and hold the traditions which you were taught, whether by word or our epistle.

2 THESSALONIANS 2:15

When Paul wrote this letter to the Thessalonians, some people were teaching false things about God. They were saying God *was* what He *was not*. That sounds a bit familiar, doesn't it? False teachers abound in our society. And with the internet, their impact is both vast and instant.

Paul's advice to the Thessalonians is just as applicable to us: "Stand fast and hold the traditions which you were taught." God's message does not change. His Word is complete and nothing is to be added to it. *That* is what we should cling to—the unchanging truth of His Word. After Paul gave this advice, he then offered prayer, asking that Jesus Himself, the Lord who has loved us, would comfort and strengthen us as we try to do good for Him (vv. 16–17). Amen!

Lord, please help me stand boldly for You. Remind me that the truth of who You are is always found in Your Word.

OCTOBER 27

BEAR FRUIT

"If you abide in Me, and My words abide in you, you will ask what you desire, and it shall be done for you. By this My Father is glorified, that you bear much fruit; so you will be My disciples."

JOHN 15:7–8

Abide isn't a word we use a lot these days, which can make "abide in Me" a bit tricky to understand. The New Living Translation puts it this way: "remain in me." So these verses simply mean that our lives—the way we think, speak, and act—need to remain, or *abide*, in the ways Jesus has said. Specifically we seek to love God and love our neighbor in all we do (Matthew 22:37–39).

But living out the love of Jesus in today's world requires the power of God. And how do we tap into His power? By praying for His guidance and strength. By studying His Word for its wisdom. By submitting our own desires to His perfect will. *That* is abiding in Jesus. And when we abide, we will "bear much fruit" for His kingdom.

Father, when I get caught up in the rush,
remind me to abide in You.

OCTOBER 28

OBEDIENCE BRINGS PEACE

"Obey me, and I will be your God, and you will be my people. Do everything as I say, and all will be well!"

JEREMIAH 7:23 NLT

Obedience is the response every parent wants from a child. When children are obedient to parental discipline and guidance, peace reigns in the home. The same is true with our heavenly Father. When we obey our Father's commands, follow His leading, and accept His correction, we are blessed with His peace—regardless of the circumstances we may find ourselves in. God promises that "all will be well." We may not understand how or when, where or why, but God will take care of those who follow Him.

Therefore, let God's Word be your daily guide and allow His Spirit to speak to your heart. Obey what He commands in His Word. Then you will enjoy His lordship, and peace will reign in your life.

Father, Your commands bring life and peace. Strengthen my resolve to obey You that I may know Your peace.

OCTOBER 29

CREATE UNITY

"God blesses those who work for peace, for they will be called the children of God."

MATTHEW 5:9 NLT

When anger and discord become frequent visitors to your church (or family, workplace, circle of friends), peace will walk out the back door. God calls His church to be of one mind and one spirit. As a member of His church, you play a vital role in making sure this happens. While you cannot control other members, you can influence them by your example. You can either add to the strife, or you can work to make peace between those who disagree.

Accept the role God has given you, and seek to create a bond of godly love that cannot be broken. For Jesus Himself has said, "God blesses those who work for peace."

Lord, teach me to walk by faith as I try to bring unity among dissenting people.

OCTOBER 30

NO OTHER GOD

"Remember the former things of old, for I am God, and there is no other; I am God, and there is none like Me."

ISAIAH 46:9

I am God, and there is none like Me." God doesn't leave one millimeter of wiggle room in this statement. He proclaims exactly who He is and who everyone else is not. And if we have any doubts about that, we can simply "remember the former things of old."

Could any other have spoken the world into being? Certainly not some rogue bit of bacteria zapped into life. Could any other send down fire from heaven, so scorching hot that it burned up the water, the rocks, even the dust of the ground (1 Kings 18:38)? Certainly not Baal. Could any other sacrifice his own son in order to promise salvation and forgiveness of sins to any who would follow him? Certainly not.

The Lord Jehovah is God. There is no other.

Lord, let Your light so shine through me that others would see it and know I serve the one true God.

OCTOBER 31

KINDNESS IS CONTAGIOUS

"What man is there among you who, if his son asks for bread, will give him a stone? . . . How much more will your Father who is in heaven give good things to those who ask Him!"

MATTHEW 7:9, 11

People with kind and tender hearts are magnets not only to those they love, but to all they encounter. Everyone, no matter how crusty or gruff, craves love and encouragement. When we demonstrate our love for others through the kind acts of a caring heart, we begin to build a relationship, a sense of confidence and security, and a foundation of trust that will not easily be broken. That will then enable us to share the love and light of our Lord.

As God demonstrates His love, grace, and mercy to you each day, so let your words and actions daily reflect that same love, grace, and mercy to each person you encounter today.

Lord Jesus, when I think of all the ways You show Your love to me, I'm inspired to show love as well. Remind me to do that today.

NOVEMBER

NOVEMBER 1

DOERS ARE BLESSED

Don't just listen to God's word. You must do what it says. . . . Then God will bless you.

JAMES 1:22, 25 NLT

It is not enough to hear the Word or to quote it in the face of the world. Even the devil can do that. To be true followers of God, we must follow His Word.

The Bible is no ordinary book to be read and then stuck back on a shelf. It is our treasure, given to us by God. We must approach it with an open heart, asking the Holy Spirit of God to reveal its riches to us.

As we look into the mirror of God's truth, it shows us our flaws and weaknesses, those things we need to do and to change. We must not then close its pages and forget what it has revealed (vv. 23–24). We must act on what it says. *Then* we will be blessed.

Lord, help me be a doer of the Word and not a hearer only. Reveal what I need to change so I may always honor You.

NOVEMBER 2

NEIGHBOR-LOVE

"Love your neighbor as yourself. I am the Lord."

LEVITICUS 19:18 NLT

The love of God and the love of those created in His image form the backbone of everything God says in His Word. When the attitude of love for your neighbor becomes part of your everyday life, caring about others becomes a natural outpouring of God's desire for those who are part of His family.

God cares for you, so let His love flow from you to your neighbors—for "everyone who loves the Father loves his children, too" (1 John 5:1 NLT). When you as a Christian demonstrate the love of God to your neighbors, you become the person God wishes you to be. If you have a neighbor who is tough to love, ask God for His help. He will always bless your efforts to obey Him.

Father, grow in me a natural love for my neighbors. I want to be a person who pleases You.

NOVEMBER 3

RICH FAITH, FLOWING LOVE

Your faith is flourishing and your love for one another is growing.

2 THESSALONIANS 1:3 NLT

When learning about God becomes a part of your daily habit, your love for His Word will naturally grow—as will your character, your faith, and your Christian walk. God's Word is essential for your Christian development. As you dwell in the Word, your faith grows rich and your love for others flows.

The more you study God's Word, the more you will find it reflected in the created world around you—"The heavens declare the glory of God" (Psalm 19:1). The intricacy of a wildflower, the perfection of a sunrise could only be the work of almighty God. Nature can open your eyes to spiritual truth in a way nothing else does. Take time to notice the power of God's presence all around you, and let your faith and love grow.

Lord, teach me through Your Word and the loveliness that surrounds me. Please grow my faith and love.

NOVEMBER 4

THE LORD SETS US ON HIGH

"Because he has set his love upon Me, therefore I will deliver him; I will set him on high, because he has known My name."

PSALM 91:14

When we love God, He protects us from want and evil. He sets us "on high." The Lord is our Deliverer, Refuge, and Shield (vv. 3–4). And when we make Him our dwelling place—when we live turning to and abiding in Him—His angels stand guard around us, protecting us from evil (vv. 9–11).

When we feel threatened, afraid, alone, let's remember the the Lord God Almighty. He shepherds us (Psalm 23:1), provides for our eternal salvation (John 3:16), sanctifies us (John 17:17), and stays close in every circumstance (Hebrews 13:5). He also promises to keep us safely in His care "on high."

Lord, I will sing Your praises from my place "on high."

NOVEMBER 5

OUR EVERLASTING HOPE

O Lord, you alone are my hope. I've trusted you, O LORD, from childhood.

PSALM 71:5 NLT

You will face certain challenges and times when the circumstances of life will test your faith. But God has promised, through His abundant mercy, that you have a living and eternal hope (1 Peter 1:3) in Jesus Christ, and no one and no thing—no challenge or circumstance—can take that hope away.

The writer of Psalm 71 held fast to this hope and had maintained his faith "from childhood." When enemies came, when troubles threatened, when age weakened, he still declared the wondrous works of the Lord (v. 17). God will honor all His promises. Even when you find yourself in seemingly hopeless situations, know that God loves you and He will make something beautiful out of your life. Keep trusting. Keep hoping. God is everlastingly faithful.

Father, in You I have time-proven hope. Thank You.

NOVEMBER 6

SORROW TURNS TO JOY

"You now have sorrow; but I will see you again and your heart will rejoice, and your joy no one will take from you."

JOHN 16:22

In John 16, Jesus was preparing His disciples for His coming death and return to heaven. Having walked side by side with these men, Jesus knew His leaving would cause them great sorrow. But He also knew that sorrow would turn to joy when they saw Him after the resurrection. That joy would not be for them alone, but for all who would choose to walk side by side with their Savior.

The joy Jesus mentioned is one that brightens times of happiness and infuses even our deepest sorrows with His hope and promises. It's a joy that nothing and no one can take away. It's a joy only God can grant and sustain, and it is His gift to us. He promises.

Lord, when pain casts a long shadow, remind me afresh of Your joy, of Your promises, of the hope of heaven with You.

NOVEMBER 7

A NEW SONG

He has put a new song in my mouth—praise to our God;
many will see it and fear, and will trust in the LORD.

PSALM 40:3

Music is a powerful thing. It expresses our thoughts and feelings in ways that words alone cannot. And so often the songs we listen to and sing are the ones that reflect the way we are feeling. In times of joy, happy melodies fill the air. But in times of sadness, we sing songs of sorrow.

When the playlist of your life seems to be stuck on the melancholy station, remember this promise from the Master Composer: He will put a new song in your mouth. He will turn your mourning into dancing (Psalm 30:11) and your sorrows into joy (John 16:20).

Call out to Him; He will hear (v. 1). Trust in Him; He will lift you up (v. 2). And He will give you a new song to sing—a song of joyful praise to your King.

Lord, I praise You—for listening, for loving, for giving me so many reasons to sing joyfully.

NOVEMBER 8

NO GREATER LOVE

"This is My commandment, that you love one another as I have loved you. Greater love has no one than this, than to lay down one's life for his friends."

JOHN 15:12–13

During His time with His disciples, Jesus commanded them—and us—to love God with all their hearts, souls, minds, and strength, and to love their neighbors as themselves (Luke 10:27). He even went so far as to say they should love their enemies (Luke 6:27). All bold statements, even radical. But this commandment was the most radical yet: to love as *He* loved.

Jesus loved tirelessly, with humility, serving unceasingly, even giving up His life for His friends. And today that kind of love marks Jesus' followers as modern-day disciples. Our love reflects our Savior's selfless love and by this we draw others to Him.

Lord, help me love as You love—tirelessly and with humility and service. I lay down my life for You.

NOVEMBER 9

LET PEACE RULE

Let the peace that comes from Christ rule in your hearts. For as members of one body you are called to live in peace.

COLOSSIANS 3:15 NLT

Life in this fallen world can provide much to worry about. Add to that humankind's propensity to focus on all the what-ifs, and your thoughts can actually fuel the fire of worry. Satan will use worry to cause doubts, confusion, and insecurity. He will also use your worries to keep you focused on circumstances rather than on God and His faithfulness.

Freedom from worry can come when you choose to think about God's truth—however contrary to reality it seems—rather than on whatever is prompting you to worry. Focusing on God's Word and His power will replace your worry with peace. After all, you are a child of the King, and you are called to let peace "rule." God promises this is possible!

Lord, when my problems grow huge, it's so easy for my faith to shrink. But I put my hope in You. Help me live in peace.

NOVEMBER 10

GOD BLESSES OUR GIVING

"Give, and it will be given to you. A good measure, pressed down, shaken together and running over, will be poured into your lap."

LUKE 6:38 NIV

God doesn't need our money. He can run the world—He can run all of creation—without our financial aid. But God wants us to trust Him, and our giving to Him of our time, talents, and treasures shows that we trust Him.

King David sang, "Give to the LORD the glory due His name; bring an offering, and come before Him. Oh, worship the LORD in the beauty of holiness!" (1 Chronicles 16:29). When we give to God, He blesses us. And when we trust Him to be our ultimate Provider, we don't need to cling to our money. He promises to richly supply all our needs (Philippians 4:19).

Giving to support God's work is one way we worship our good and generous heavenly Father—and He blesses our giving.

Lord, show me how and what You would like me to give.

NOVEMBER 11

WHAT YOU DO MATTERS

You were not redeemed with corruptible things, like silver or gold, from your aimless conduct received by tradition from your fathers, but with the precious blood of Christ.

1 PETER 1:18–19

We are to honor Jesus with all we do and say. Not only because of all He has given us—mercy, grace, and salvation—but also because of all He gave up for us—the wonders of heaven, the presence of His Father, His own precious blood. But honoring Jesus is no easy task in today's world.

Some might argue that what one mere person says or does could be of little importance to the God of heaven. But they would be wrong. Our Lord notices our every word and step. He knows our every thought before we think it. God knows and notices—because what we do and say matters to Him. We bring Him glory when we obey—and honor—Him.

I am so thankful for the sacrifice You made for me, Jesus. Teach me to bring honor and glory to Your name.

NOVEMBER 12

A SOFT ANSWER

A soft answer turns away wrath, but a harsh word stirs up anger.

PROVERBS 15:1

As prickly as a cactus. It's an old saying used to describe those people who just seem to go through life poking, jabbing, and stabbing at others. Some we can easily avoid, like that testy clerk at the grocery store. Others aren't so easily avoided, like certain family members and yes, even some of our fellow believers. What's a peace-loving Christian to do?

First, pray. Ask God to set a guard upon your lips (Psalm 141:3), so you don't make things even worse and so you can indeed take the next step, which is to offer that soft answer. The promised effect may not be immediate, but gradually, over time, your soft words will smooth away those prickly edges, just as water smooths the sharp stone. It isn't easy, but you will have the joy of knowing you've fulfilled Jesus' command to turn the other cheek (Matthew 5:39).

Lord, when others prick me with their words, fill my mind and my mouth with Your soft answer.

NOVEMBER 13

THE RESTLESS FIND PEACE

Be joyful. Grow to maturity. Encourage each other. Live in harmony and peace.

2 CORINTHIANS 13:11 NLT

The realities of life can be unsettling. Responsibilities can weigh heavily. Trials and tribulations can bring uncertainty and even hopelessness. Seemingly impossible situations can be puzzling. Much in this world can try to rob you of peace.

You can prevent that robbery when you choose to trust in the Lord, when you decide to remember His faithfulness throughout the year, and when you focus on the truth of His sovereignty, His unlimited power, and His unshakable love for you.

If you are feeling restless, choose to trust in the Lord today. Seek harmony. Embrace the lasting peace only He can promise and only He can give.

Lord, thank You for lifting the burden of restlessness from me. Cover me with Your grace and peace.

NOVEMBER 14

THE BOOK OF LIFE

"He who overcomes shall be clothed in white garments, and I will not blot out his name from the Book of Life; but I will confess his name before My Father and before His angels."

REVELATION 3:5

Your name appears in a lot of places: in yearbooks and phone books and address books, on bank statements and bills, perhaps even on a trophy or two. But there is no place more important or more glorious for your name to appear than in the Book of Life.

When we place our trust in the Lord and in His Son, we are given the gift of salvation—not because of anything we have done, but because of the great love and mercy of our Lord. Then our names will be written in the Book of Life, and when Jesus returns, we will hear Him read our names before the Father and all of heaven's angels. And that will be just the beginning of a glorious eternity with Him.

Thank You, Lord, for writing my name in Your great Book of Life. I cannot wait for You to read my name!

NOVEMBER 15

THIS IS THE WAY

Your ears shall hear a word behind you, saying, "This is the way, walk in it," whenever you turn to the right hand or whenever you turn to the left.

ISAIAH 30:21

God doesn't play games with His people. Just the opposite is true. When we search for the Lord with all our hearts, He promises to be found (Jeremiah 29:13).

In His Word, we can find everything we need to know to please Him, to show our love for Him, to live lives that honor Him. As we diligently study His words, asking the Holy Spirit to open their meaning to us, we draw near to the heart of God—and He draws near to us (James 4:8). So near that when we face those decisions, when we stand at those crossroads in our lives, we can hear Him clearly whisper, "This is the way, walk in it."

Lord, there are so many decisions and choices. Remind me to turn to You and Your Word, to listen as You tell me the way to go.

NOVEMBER 16

INFINITE UNDERSTANDING

Great is our Lord, and mighty in power;
His understanding is infinite.

PSALM 147:5

If you are a parent, you know how hard it is to see your child upset and fearful. Similarly, your loving heavenly Father longs for you to be at peace rather than upset, fearful, and stressed. The best way to deal with your stress—to be rid of it—is to run to the Lord.

One way to do that is by spending time in prayer and focusing on His unshakable love for you. Scripture declares that God is "mighty in power" and has unlimited understanding. Focus on that for a moment: Scripture promises that God understands whatever it is you're thinking, feeling, experiencing—and He has the power to help you. He wants to exchange your stress for His peace.

> Lord, You know all I'm facing. Please reassure me with Your presence and comfort me with Your peace.

NOVEMBER 17

WE LACK NOTHING

Those who seek the Lord shall not lack any good thing.

PSALM 34:10

The loss of a job can shake a wage earner to the very core. An illness can devastate family finances. Unexpected expenses can send you reeling. You may have learned these lessons from experience, or you may be experiencing one of them right now. What are you going to do to pay the bills and feed your family? You might also be wondering why God allowed this to happen. If you are, then turn to Him and ask, "What do You want me to learn from this?"

God is always teaching His children to trust Him. So choose to believe that the Lord knows your needs. Turn to Him, spend time with Him, and seek His perfect will for your life.

God will work everything out for the best (Romans 8:28). Rest in His presence and choose, moment by moment, to trust Him. His Word promises you shall lack nothing.

Lord, You bless my life with all I truly need. Thank You, Lord!

NOVEMBER 18

POWER FOR THE WEAK

Be of good courage, and He shall strengthen your heart, all you who hope in the LORD.

PSALM 31:24

Pain in this world often comes from misplaced confidence—when we place our trust in anyone or anything other than the Lord, including ourselves. If we've been relying on our strength to see us through, only to discover we can't do it all on our own, our confidence plummets. Family challenges, business disappointments, financial pressure, and even a bad night's sleep can then send us spiraling further downward.

In times like these, we must stop trusting in ourselves and put our confidence in the almighty God. After all, He has promised to be with us always (Matthew 28:20) and in every circumstance. He has promised never to leave or forsake us (Hebrews 13:5). And He has promised that He will strengthen our hearts.

Lord, I look forward to Your turning around this painful situation and empowering me.

NOVEMBER 19

EVERLASTING MERCY

The mercy of the Lord *is from everlasting to everlasting on those who fear Him, and His righteousness to children's children.*

PSALM 103:17

If you have children in your life, you know how precious they are, and you want only the best for them. You pray that they grow up to love the Lord and live fruitful lives in His kingdom. Unfortunately, your children may disappoint you. Be patient with them just as God, your heavenly Father, is patient with you. The way you react when you're disappointed in them will reveal much about your own relationship with God. Make sure they see His love reflected in you.

Your loving response will also enable you to help them to face their mistakes and the consequences that follow. Turn to God for His wisdom and guidance as you seek to discipline and correct your children. Remember, the mercy of the Lord is everlasting, just like His love (Jeremiah 31:3). So let yours be also.

Lord, let my reaction to disappointments—of any kind—always reflect my love for You.

NOVEMBER 20

GOD REMEMBERS

The Lord *. . . has remembered His mercy and His faithfulness.*

PSALM 98:2–3

We forget so many things: birthdays, anniversaries, what we had for breakfast. But God doesn't. God remembers.

He remembers our names—they're written on the palms of His hands (Isaiah 49:16); our tears (Psalm 56:8); every hair on our heads (Luke 12:7). Drink those verses in. Let them seep into your soul and saturate your heart. The One who spoke just four little words and sent light blazing through the universe . . . He remembers *you*. And not only does He remember you, He sends so many loving and merciful thoughts toward you they cannot even be counted (Psalm 40:5)!

We forget so many things. Sometimes we even forget our Lord. But He never forgets. Yes, God remembers you.

Lord, to be known and loved and remembered by You is the greatest of blessings. Let me love and honor You too.

NOVEMBER 21

UNENDING GOODNESS

I would have lost heart, unless I had believed that I would see the goodness of the LORD in the land of the living.

PSALM 27:13

References to the goodness of God appear throughout the Bible, and that shouldn't surprise us. After all, what other kind of God would be faithful to such faithless ones as us? Would any God but a good God be patient with us in our sin, generous in His provision for us, or constant in His love?

And God's goodness is not at all weak: He is all-powerful and all-wise as He showers His children with blessings. Even when He doesn't approve of our decisions and actions, even as He waits for us to walk with Him wholeheartedly, our good God provides for us. His ever-present goodness keeps us from losing heart in the rough and tumble of this sin-filled world. God is good, and He daily blesses us with His goodness.

Lord, You are such a good God—and I am so thankful that Your goodness doesn't depend on mine. Open my eyes to Your generosity all around me.

NOVEMBER 22

GOD NEVER BETRAYS US

You have been my help; do not leave me nor forsake me, O God of my salvation. When my father and my mother forsake me, then the Lord *will take care of me.*

PSALM 27:9–10

Trust can take a long time to grow and solidify, yet it can disappear in an instant. You may be dealing with the pain of having someone you loved and trusted abandon or betray you. As you grieve and cope with your loss, remember that your compassionate God is at your side. *Always.* And He has promised that He will never leave or forsake you. *Never.*

Turn to your heavenly Father, rest in His presence, and believe His commitment to love you with an everlasting love. Since God is for you, who can be against you (Romans 8:31)? Though all others fail, God will take care of you. He promises!

I will praise You, Lord, all the days of my life.
Thank You for Your endless faithfulness.

NOVEMBER 23

WORTHY OF PRAISE

Praise Him for His mighty acts; praise Him according to His excellent greatness!

PSALM 150:2

Praising the Lord in all life's situations is a healthy expression of God's never-ending love for each of us. Through our praise and His Spirit, God gives us the ability to face whatever life may bring. While it's easy to sing His praises when life is running smoothly, it's when things are less than ideal that our praises are most needed. Not for God, but for ourselves. Proclaiming His power and greatness reminds us He truly is in control and is working all things for our good (Romans 8:28).

When we praise Him, we declare our trust in His absolute authority. And the sense of security that only He can give will fill our hearts and minds, and give us that promised peace that passes all understanding (Philippians 4:7).

Lord, I do praise You—in the good times, bad times, and all the everyday times in between. You are Lord of all.

NOVEMBER 24

HE HEARS AND HEALS

"If My people who are called by My name will humble themselves, and pray and seek My face, and turn from their wicked ways, then I will hear from heaven, and will forgive their sin and heal their land."

2 CHRONICLES 7:14

It's a crazy world . . . and it seems to be getting crazier by the minute. Words like *tolerance*, *justice*, and *equality* have been stretched to mean things they were never meant to mean, to encompass ideals they were never meant to embrace. And standing up for our beliefs can lead to job loss, lawsuits, or even closing our business. As believers, it can be both overwhelming and discouraging. What are we to do?

God tells us exactly what to do: humble ourselves, pray, and seek His face, removing any wickedness from our lives. He will hear our cries. He will forgive our sins. And when the time is right, He will heal the land of His people.

Lord, when this world seems to be spinning out of control, help me remember that You are still Lord over all.

NOVEMBER 25

THE CROWN OF LIFE

Blessed is the man who endures temptation; for when he has been approved, he will receive the crown of life which the Lord has promised to those who love Him.

JAMES 1:12

These verses from James address the unpleasant and gritty reality of living in a fallen world. There *will* be temptations. And when facing them, we have two choices—to endure, relying on the strength and power of our Lord, or to succumb. Giving in to temptation leads to sin. But standing strong, staying true to God and His will, leads to victory and the crown of life.

God wants to give each and every one of us that crown of life. He is *not* the one tempting us (v. 13); rather, it is the evil one who prowls around like a roaring lion (1 Peter 5:8). But in His Word and with His Spirit, God has given us everything we need to resist. And then He crowns us with an eternal life in heaven with Him.

Lord, strengthen me in the times of temptation. I look forward to wearing the crown of life.

NOVEMBER 26

GOD REWARDS THE WAITING

God made a promise to Abraham . . . saying, "Surely blessing I will bless you, and multiplying I will multiply you." And so, after he had patiently endured, he obtained the promise.

HEBREWS 6:13–15

Twenty-five years. That's how long Abraham waited for God to keep His promise. More than two decades passed before Isaac, the promised son, was born. Abraham never forgot God's promise. And he waited (though imperfectly) for God to fulfill it. He never gave up on God, turned his back on Him, or declared God was not willing or able to do what He had said He would do. Abraham waited, and God rewarded his waiting.

He will always take care of us, He will provide for us, He will save us from our enemies, and He will lead us home. But He may also ask us to wait. And when we wait, believing He will keep His word, God rewards us by doing just that.

Father, when I grow weary of waiting, remind me that Your way and Your timing will be exactly what I need.

NOVEMBER 27

GOD'S WORD ENDURES

Love one another fervently with a pure heart, having been born again, not of corruptible seed but incorruptible, through the word of God which lives and abides forever.

1 PETER 1:22–23

The word of God . . . lives and abides forever." What comfort in this world where things change so quickly and so dramatically!

In this passage Peter encourages us to love our fellow believers "fervently with a pure heart." This is no easy task, as you know. Even believers are still human, with all their tendencies to sin and offend. But we are enabled to do this because we have been born again through God's unchanging Word.

As we meditate upon God's Word, it continues to teach us, to strengthen us, to empower us to do God's will every day. No matter what may come in this world, what struggles or trials we face, we can know that God's Word will abide forever.

Father, through Your Word and Your Son I have been made Your child. Teach me to love my brothers and sisters in Christ.

NOVEMBER 28

ARMOR OF GOD

Be strong in the Lord and in the power of His might. Put on the whole armor of God, that you may be able to stand against the wiles of the devil.

EPHESIANS 6:10–11

Satan is no mythical creature, no red-suited cartoon character; he is alive and busy. His influences can be seen every time we put ourselves first, every time we shortcut the truth with a little white lie, every time we betray another to get ahead. We all must fight the battle against temptation.

But God doesn't leave us defenseless for the fight. He offers us His spiritual armor and then commands us to put it on—to gird ourselves with His truth, His righteousness, and His gospel of peace. We are to take up the shield of faith, strap on the helmet of salvation, and lift up the sword of God's Word. When we allow God to protect us, no weapon the devil forms against us will stand (Isaiah 54:17).

Father, teach me to use Your armor, and strengthen me for the fight.

NOVEMBER 29

GOD STAYS WITH US

"Behold, I am with you and will keep you wherever you go, and will bring you back to this land; for I will not leave you until I have done what I have spoken to you."

GENESIS 28:15

Behold, I am with you." These were the words, the promise, God spoke to Jacob. Notice that God not only promised Jacob His presence but also His protection. Our God is not just a God who walks alongside us in this life, He is a God who intervenes to help, to shield, to guide—even to fight our battles for us, when needed (Exodus 14:14).

But let's put God's promises to Jacob into context. When God spoke these words to Jacob, he had stolen his brother Esau's blessing and was running away to hide out with relatives until his brother's anger cooled. Yet God said He was with Jacob. The promise for us then is this: on the treacherous waves of life, even the ones we create for ourselves, God is still with us.

Father, I am so thankful that You do not abandon me in the storms, even the ones I make myself.

NOVEMBER 30

LONELY NO MORE

"Lo, I am with you always, even to the end of the age."

MATTHEW 28:20

Loneliness can weigh down your heart, erode your confidence, and rob you of hope. If that's where you are right now, consider this: Jesus Himself was lonely when, early in His ministry, His family didn't understand Him. Jesus was lonely when His disciples were slow to recognize Him and slow to understand why He had come. And Jesus undoubtedly felt very much alone when Judas betrayed Him and Peter denied knowing Him.

Jesus understands our loneliness, and He promises never to leave us alone, "even to the end of the age." When loneliness overtakes you, turn to Jesus, the One who is with you throughout every day and every night. In Him you'll find the sweetest companionship you'll ever know.

Lord, sometimes this life can be lonely, so I thank You for Your constant presence.

DECEMBER

DECEMBER 1

CLOSE TO HIS HEART

He gathers the lambs in his arms and carries them close to his heart.

ISAIAH 40:11 NIV

Some days . . . you just need a hug. It doesn't even have to be a terrible day. Perhaps it's just an ordinary Tuesday or a Saturday afternoon, but you need someone to remind you that you really are loved, that you really are important, and that you're not on this journey alone.

Read again these beautiful words from Isaiah: "He gathers the lambs in his arms and carries them close to his heart." Dear child of God, *you* are His lamb. *You* are the one He gathers into His arms. *You* are the one He carries close to His heart. Listen to Him as His Spirit whispers truth to your heart: you are so loved (John 3:16), you are so important to Him (1 John 3:1), and you are never, ever alone (Matthew 28:20).

Lord, thank You for Your love that is so great and so personal and so perfect for me. I will hold You close to my heart always, just as You hold me.

DECEMBER 2

GOD WILL RENEW YOU

For our light affliction, which is but for a moment, is working for us a far more exceeding and eternal weight of glory.

2 CORINTHIANS 4:17

God has a plan for our lives, and it's overflowing with the abundance of His blessings. Yet we still experience anxiety and affliction because we live in a world beset with sin. And though the daily battles of this world may wear us down, may make us feel older, "tireder," weaker, we do not give up (v. 16). We arise each morning to another day and another opportunity to serve and bring glory to our God. We are able to do this because each day our spirit is strengthened, restored, and renewed by the One who loves us so much He sent His own Son to save us.

Any sorrow we suffer, any wound we bear is but a "light affliction," lasting only "for a moment" when compared with the eternity of heaven promised to those who love the Lord.

Father, when troubles overwhelm, remind me that they will pass and You will always remain.

DECEMBER 3

STAND ON THE WORD

The grass withers, the flower fades, but the word of our God stands forever.

ISAIAH 40:8

The "truths" of this world are ever changing. What was once wrong is now declared right, while what was once right is now declared wrong. If we try to build our lives on the truths of this world, we will—like that man whose house stood on the shifting sands—soon find ourselves floundering in the winds and storms of life. But God's Word does not change; its truths stand forever. And when we build our lives on its solid foundation, we will—like the man who build his house upon the rock—be found still standing, even amid the storms (Matthew 7:24–27).

The Word offers us all the information we need, but the choice is still ours: trust it and live wisely, or discard it and live foolishly. Only one option gives us a solid foundation.

So many things come and go, but You, Lord, never leave or change. I will make You my foundation for life.

DECEMBER 4

FOUND BLAMELESS

Fight the good fight of faith, lay hold on eternal life. . . .
Keep this commandment without spot, blameless
until our Lord Jesus Christ's appearing.

1 TIMOTHY 6:12, 14

Paul urged Timothy—and us—to fight the good fight of faith. What does that mean? It means to flee all evil things and to "pursue righteousness, godliness, faith, love, patience, gentleness" (v. 11). In other words, we live our lives honoring Christ in everything we say and do.

At times living faithfully can feel like a battle. The devil our adversary prowls around like a lion, looking for an opportunity to snare and devour us (1 Peter 5:8). Thankfully the Holy Spirit of God is ever with us, lighting the way and shielding us with God's Word. When we obey this command to fight the good fight, we are blessed with the mercy and grace of God. Then when we appear before Him, we will be found blameless.

Lord, help me keep Your commandments without spot so I may win the good fight of faith.

DECEMBER 5

A HOME WITH GOD

Even the sparrow finds a home, and the swallow builds her nest and raises her young at a place near your altar, O LORD of Heaven's Armies, my King and my God!

PSALM 84:3 NLT

A home with God—is there any thought more lovely, more comforting, more sustaining? Yes, one day we will be free of this life and its turmoil. As beloved children of God, we will be blessed to join Him in our forever home in heaven.

But we don't have to wait for heaven to find our home with God. Psalm 84 tells us that even the sparrow and the swallow have found a home, a place to nest near His altar, where they are ever under His watchful care (Matthew 10:29). So we, being much more precious to Him than the sparrows (v. 31), need not wait for heaven to find a home with God. We can dwell in His presence today—singing His praises our whole lives through.

Lord, *home* makes me think of warmth and welcome and love; it makes me think of You. Thank You for being my home.

DECEMBER 6

SECURE IN OUR LORD

The Lord shall preserve you from all evil; He shall preserve your soul. The Lord shall preserve your going out and your coming in from this time forth, and even forevermore.

PSALM 121:7–8

God helps, protects, and guides those who seek Him with all their hearts. Though He never promises that this life will be free of hardship or pain, He promises to walk with us each moment, allowing us to lean upon His strength, draw from His courage, and be led by His wisdom. And He insists that the souls of those who know and love Him will be preserved—no matter what troubles come.

God *surrounds* those who love Him, like a thick wall surrounding an ancient city. He covers us on every side so that nothing reaches us without first passing through His loving hands. We are safe and secure in our Lord.

Lord, thank You for wrapping me in the security of Your love and presence. I know I am safe with You.

DECEMBER 7

ALL GOD'S PROMISES

The Lord always keeps his promises; he is gracious in all he does.

PSALM 145:13 NLT

Through God's promises, we can not only walk through our faith-life without growing weary, we can soar (Isaiah 40:31). He blesses us with His wisdom (James 1:5) and sends evil packing (James 4:7). When we confess our sins, He faithfully forgives us (1 John 1:9). He seals us with His Spirit, guaranteeing us a home and an inheritance in heaven (2 Corinthians 1:22). All these promises and more are utterly reliable because of Jesus. As Paul wrote, "All of God's promises have been fulfilled in Christ with a resounding 'Yes!' And through Christ, our 'Amen' (which means 'Yes') ascends to God for his glory" (2 Corinthians 1:20 NLT).

Because the Lord "always keeps his promises," let's shout "Yes" and "Amen" to the glory of God!

Lord, when I think of all Your promises, I am in awe of Your lovingkindness. I praise You for sending Your Son to keep them all.

DECEMBER 8

EVERY WORD

I love the Lord because he hears my voice and my prayer for mercy. Because he bends down to listen, I will pray as long as I have breath!

PSALM 116:1–2 NLT

"I love the Lord." What a beautiful way to begin a praise, a new day, each moment of our lives! And then the psalmist begins to tell us why: God listens (v. 1), saves (v. 6), preserves (v. 6), delivers (v. 8), and sets us free (v. 16).

But it's the heartwarming promise found in verse 2 that gives us a glimpse of the personal relationship God so longs to have with His children. "Because he bends down to listen." What a beautiful image, the almighty God—Lord and Ruler of All—*bends down to listen as we pray*. Just imagine . . . God not only invites us to pray whenever, wherever, and about whatever we want, but He leans over, to get just a little closer, to make sure He doesn't miss a word of what we have to say.

Holy Father, just the thought of You bending down to listen to me fills me with awe and joy and praise. Thank You for loving me so.

DECEMBER 9

JESUS IS WILLING

A man who was full of leprosy saw Jesus; and he fell on his face and implored Him, saying, "Lord, if You are willing, You can make me clean." Then He put out His hand and touched him, saying, "I am willing; be cleansed."

LUKE 5:12–13

In the days of Jesus, a leper could not be touched. Sheer survival became complicated—how to work, get food, provide for yourself and a family when no one could touch you. But there were also the daily heartbreaks: no hugs, no tender touches, not even a passing pat on the back.

Which makes what Jesus did all the more extraordinary. Yes, He healed the leper, but look at what He did first: Jesus *touched* him. *Then* the man was made clean, because Jesus was willing. We are so much like that leper, made untouchable by our sins. But Jesus does the extraordinary. He touches us with His grace, cleansing us of all sin . . . because He is willing. It's why He came.

O Lord Jesus, touch me, cleanse me, make me wholly and forever Yours.

DECEMBER 10

BEGINNING AND END

"I am the Alpha and the Omega, the Beginning and the End. I will give of the fountain of the water of life freely to him who thirsts. He who overcomes shall inherit all things."

REVELATION 21:6–7

Alpha and *Omega*. *Beginning* and *End*. Such regal, awe-inspiring words to describe our regal and awe-inspiring God. And though they speak of His vast power, His omniscient knowledge, and His all-encompassing presence, they also give a deeper, more personal message: God is, was, and will always be. He does not leave; He does not change. He *is*.

And He knit us together in our mothers' wombs (Psalm 139:13), knew our days before ever there was one (Psalm 139:16), and holds our future in His loving hands (Jeremiah 29:11). There is no place we can go where He is not, no time when He is not. And when we surrender our will and our ways to Him, He invites us to drink freely from the fountain of life and promises that we shall indeed "inherit all things."

Lord, You *are* . . . and that is enough for me.

DECEMBER 11

PURE WISDOM

Every word of God is pure; He is a shield to those who put their trust in Him.

PROVERBS 30:5

When we accept the promise that "every word of God is pure," that it can be fully trusted, then our entire lives begin to change. We see ourselves, this world, and all that happens in it through the lens of His unchanging truth. And we see that we have a mighty and impenetrable Shield who protects our souls from this world and all that happens in it.

The Word of God holds every answer, but we must be careful to keep it pure. No matter what we might hear, or what a preacher or speaker may say, we must take everything and compare it to God's true Word—rejecting anything that does not perfectly align. Only God's Word is pure; only God's Word is reliable; only God's Word is truth. Trust only in His given Word.

Lord, I know every word in Your Scripture is pure and comes from You. Help me discern Your truth from others' ideas.

DECEMBER 12

GOD IS GOOD

The Lord is good, a stronghold in the day of trouble;
and He knows those who trust in Him.

NAHUM 1:7

Though we call many things in this world *good*, none of them is *perfectly* good. But God is. There is not one spot of darkness in Him (1 John 1:5). He never lies or breaks a promise (Numbers 23:19). He sacrifices Himself to meet our needs (John 3:16). God is good . . . always.

We may not understand Him, and we certainly cannot predict His ways, but we can count on His goodness. It works in us all throughout our lives, shaping us into the image of Christ and guiding us ever closer to Him. Yes, He is "a stronghold in the day of trouble"—and we are blessed when we take refuge in Him (Psalm 34:8). But God also "knows those who trust in Him." He knows when we trust Him, however imperfectly, and He rewards us with His goodness.

Lord, please strengthen my trust by helping me to see Your goodness all around me.

DECEMBER 13

GOD'S GOOD CREATION

God saw all that he had made, and it was very good.

GENESIS 1:31 NIV

We are God's good creation. No, not perfect. We mess up and we sin—accidentally and intentionally. We lie and stretch the truth. We get selfish, we get stingy, we get caught up in the rat race.

But we are made in the image of our good and perfect God (Genesis 1:27), fearfully and wonderfully made (Psalm 139:14). Everything within us that is loving, kind, gentle, pure, and peaceable comes from our Father.

So when you look in the mirror and you see all that is wrong, don't forget all that is right. And don't forget all that God makes right—as He covers over all our imperfections with the cloak of Jesus' righteousness. You are made in the image of a good and perfect God, and He Himself declares that His creation is "very good."

Lord, teach me to see myself as You do. And please cover all my imperfections with Your righteousness.

DECEMBER 14

GOD CHOSE US

He chose us in Him before the foundation of the world, that we should be holy and without blame before Him in love.

EPHESIANS 1:4

God chose us. While we may not understand the hows and whens and whys of this choosing—at least not this side of heaven—don't miss that astounding, amazing, awesome truth. *God chose us.* Chose *you.* To be joined with Christ, to be seated with Him in heaven one day, and to be adopted into the very family of God.

Before the world was ever created, God wanted us by His side in heaven for all eternity. He knew we couldn't get there on our own, so He promised to make a way. He sent His Son so we could be "holy and without fault in his eyes" (NLT). God chose us—the question then is, *Have we chosen Him?*

You chose me, Lord, to be by Your side—and went to extraordinary lengths to make sure it was possible. With all my life, I praise You!

DECEMBER 15

SUN AND SHIELD

The Lord *God is a sun and shield; the* Lord *will give grace and glory; no good thing will He withhold from those who walk uprightly.*

PSALM 84:11

Psalm 84:11 is filled with promises for "those who walk uprightly."

First, the Lord is our Sun. He not only sustains us with the warmth of His love, He also lights our way through the darkness we encounter. The Lord is also our Shield, protecting us from the vicious attacks of the evil one. He gives us grace we do not deserve and teaches us to live for His glory.

The one who walks uprightly is the one who chooses the Lord above all else. As the psalmist said, "I would rather be a doorkeeper in the house of my God than dwell in the tents of wickedness" (v. 10). From such a one, God will withhold no good thing.

Lord, my Sun and Shield, thank You for Your grace and goodness. Teach me to live for Your glory every day.

DECEMBER 16

A HEAVENLY INHERITANCE

Blessed be the God and Father of our Lord Jesus Christ, who according to His abundant mercy has begotten us again to a living hope through the resurrection of Jesus Christ from the dead, to an inheritance incorruptible . . . reserved in heaven for you.

1 PETER 1:3–4

The hope we have in God is not just a wish or a want; it is a promise waiting to be fulfilled. And it is not like the promises of man, which may or may not come to pass; God's promise is certain. What is this promise? That through the resurrection of Jesus, we are guaranteed an incorruptible inheritance, held for us in heaven.

Knowing this world is merely the beginning of a new life with Christ is the hope that keeps us going in the darkest times. And because God is faithful, we know our hope will be fulfilled—and one day we will claim our inheritance in heaven.

Lord, I take the resurrection as Your pledge to one day take me home with You. Thank You for my living hope of heaven.

DECEMBER 17

SEATED BESIDE CHRIST

God, who is rich in mercy, because of His great love with which He loved us, even when we were dead in trespasses, made us alive together with Christ.

EPHESIANS 2:4–5

God gifts us with salvation, not because of who we are or what we have done, but "because of His great love with which He loved us." He extends His mercy and grace to us when we acknowledge Christ as Savior and Lord. God's rich mercy exists because of His unfathomable goodness (Psalm 119:68).

God doesn't require perfection—not before or after we accept His grace. He sent Jesus to die for us "even when we were dead in trespasses." And after we accept His gift of salvation, His mercies still rain down upon our repentant hearts—so fully that we are lifted up and seated by the side of Christ (Ephesians 2:6).

Lord, I am nothing without You. I praise You for a grace so great that it lifts me up and seats me with Christ.

DECEMBER 18

"I WILL BE WITH YOU"

"When you pass through the waters, I will be with you; and through the rivers, they shall not overflow you. When you walk through the fire, you shall not be burned, nor shall the flame scorch you."

ISAIAH 43:2

We all have them. Those moments—those weeks or months or even years—of fiery trials, of raging floods. God never promises that we won't. In fact, just the opposite is true. We are told there will be fires to walk through, rivers of sorrow to cross, persecutions to endure.

But God will also be there. That is His promise. As His beloved children, we will never walk alone. The flame will not scorch us; the waters will not overwhelm us. The persecutions will not crush us (2 Corinthians 4:8).

Wherever we go, whatever we do, whatever we face—God will be there.

Father, You are my everything. When the fires burn, when the waters rage, I will cling to You and praise Your name.

DECEMBER 19

GOD BLESSES OUR TRUST

"The man who trusts in the Lord . . . shall be like a tree planted by the waters, which spreads out its roots by the river . . . [and] will [not] cease from yielding fruit."

JEREMIAH 17:7–8

Trust isn't always an easy thing to give. All too often, people accidentally—or not so accidentally—betray us, leaving us wary of trusting again. But God is not like us. He is not changeable. He is faithful to keep His promises. We can put our faith in Him—completely and without fear.

That doesn't mean our lives will be free from troubles or sorrows or struggles. But it does mean that God will always be faithful to help us when we need Him. When we trust in the Lord with all of our hearts, seeking His will, He will show us the way (Proverbs 3:5–6). And like a tree planted by the water, our lives can still bear fruit for His kingdom.

Lord, I do trust in You, but please strengthen me on those days when my trust wavers.

DECEMBER 20

FOR A REASON

God has set the members, each one of them,
in the body just as He pleased.

1 CORINTHIANS 12:18

You are where you are for a reason. If you like where you are, chances are you like that thought. But if you don't like where you are, well, perhaps this isn't a favorite saying of yours. And if you're in a particularly heartbreaking, difficult, or even dangerous situation, you may begin to question God, to ask, "Why?"

God is all-powerful. Nothing escapes His notice or His control. Therefore nothing comes into our lives except that which God has allowed. And we'll never fully understand why He allows some of the things He does, at least not this side of heaven. But we can know that He uses all things for our good—to teach us to persevere, to strengthen our character, to establish our hope (Romans 5:3–4). So when you don't like where you are, trust that it's for a reason and that God will use it for good.

Lord, use me—right where I am—as a shining light to lead others to You.

DECEMBER 21

GRACE FOR ALL

The Word became flesh and dwelt among us, and we beheld His glory, the glory as of the only begotten of the Father, full of grace and truth.

JOHN 1:14

The Word became flesh." The New Living Translation says, "So the Word became human and made his home among us." Jesus, our Lord and Savior, accepted an assignment . . . to be born fully human, to grow up, to know pain and sorrow, to walk through the dust and sin of this world.

Jesus came not just for the prophets and not just for the chosen nation of Israel, but for all people of all times. Jesus came for us. His love and His grace are great enough to encompass us all. The Father did not force Jesus to come. He *chose* to come, to give us the gift of His grace. Now it's up to us to choose Him in return, to accept His gift. Jesus will not force us, but He prays that we choose Him.

Father, show me afresh the power of the love and grace Jesus offered.

DECEMBER 22

THE RIGHT WAY

They cried out to the LORD in their trouble, and He delivered them out of their distresses. And He led them forth by the right way.

PSALM 107:6–7

Every day we face choices about what to do and which way to go. Some choices are clearly right or wrong, and these are easy to make. But others are more difficult, whether it's because we're not sure which choice is best or because we stubbornly long to go the very way we know is wrong.

But every day, in every area of our lives, our God is ever before us. When we turn to Him, He leads us "by the right way"—not because He must, but because He delights in doing so (Micah 7:18–19). He will direct our paths and help us rein in our wayward thoughts and control our words (Psalm 141:3). Without God, we are lost. But that's the glorious news, isn't it? As children of God, we are never without Him. So we need never be lost.

Lord, lead me in the right way, for I know that without You I would be lost.

DECEMBER 23

GOD LISTENS

Give ear to my voice when I cry out to You. Let my prayer be set before You as incense.

PSALM 141:1–2

As each new day unfolds, we are presented with both a choice and an opportunity. The choice is this: To whom will we turn for guidance, to show us the way through this life? That choice then gives us a beautiful opportunity: to turn to God in prayer.

Whether it's for praise or sadness, joy or longing, trouble or triumph, God is always ready to listen, always "near to all who call upon Him" (Psalm 145:18). And His listening is never grudging or reluctant; instead, our prayers are as incense before Him, a beautiful fragrance.

When you find yourself searching for someone to talk to, someone to listen, remember God. Call out to Him. He's never more than a whispered word away. *Lord . . .*

Lord, I come to You in prayer. Open my ears to hear Your voice and my heart to follow You.

DECEMBER 24

CHRIST MAKES US RICH

Though He was rich, yet for your sakes He became poor, that you through His poverty might become rich.

2 CORINTHIANS 8:9

What do you imagine heaven is like? With streets of gold and gates of jewels? With peace and love and joy abounding? Can you imagine ever leaving such a place?

Jesus did. Surrounded by the glories of heaven, Jesus chose to leave. He left heaven to go to the poorest people and humblest circumstances—an enslaved nation, a young bride-to-be, a poor carpenter, a manger in a stable. Why?

For our sakes.

No matter how full our bank account, we are poverty-stricken without God. For us, Jesus left heaven and made Himself poor so that we "might become rich" in God. He's offering heaven to you. All you have to do is say yes.

Jesus, You left all the wonders of heaven—for my sake. "Thank You" just isn't enough; I give my life to You.

DECEMBER 25

A SAVIOR IS GIVEN

Unto us a Child is born, unto us a Son is given. . . .
And His name will be called Wonderful, Counselor,
Mighty God, Everlasting Father, Prince of Peace.

ISAIAH 9:6

God foretold the coming of Jesus long before He came. From the foundation of the world, He knew His beloved Son would humble Himself so that His beloved—but sin-stained—people could be lifted up. Jesus would leave all the might and glory and majesty of heaven to be born an infant, a babe laid in a dusty manger. The Son of God . . . *given to us.*

Jesus is the Cornerstone upon which our faith is built, upon which all the promises of God are kept (Acts 4:11). He is Wonderful, the Counselor who comforts and guides us. He is our Mighty God, fully divine. And as the Prince of Peace, He brings our hearts a peace that passes all understanding today and a home of eternal peace in heaven. All because a Savior is born unto us.

Lord, thank You for giving us Your Son.

DECEMBER 26

PERFECTLY FORGIVEN

All we like sheep have gone astray; we have turned, every one, to his own way; and the Lord has laid on Him the iniquity of us all.

ISAIAH 53:6

God's children—His sheep—are prone to wandering. Not one of us is exempt from it, though some might pretend to be. The truth is that we have all, at one point or another, gone astray and turned to our own way.

God could have written off His silly sheep. He could have thrown up His hands and said, "Enough already! I've told them exactly what to do and still they don't do it!" But He didn't. Instead God took all our sins and laid them on His innocent Son. Through Jesus' sacrifice, God offers His wandering sheep a way to come home. He truly forgives all our sins when we repent and surrender ourselves to His perfect will.

God sent His Son because He knows His children aren't perfect, but we can be perfectly forgiven.

Lord, You sent Your Son to pay for my sins, and I thank You for that beautiful gift.

DECEMBER 27

WE WILL SHINE

"Let your light so shine before men, that they may see your good works and glorify your Father in heaven."

MATTHEW 5:16

A candle in the dark night of a power outage . . . a flashlight in a cave . . . a word of truth in a world of lies and spin and propaganda.

As each of these scenarios suggests, a little light can have a huge impact on a situation. Similarly, we who love Jesus can't help but shine with His light. And we must not try to cover it up—don't hide it under a basket (Matthew 5:15) for fear of what the world might say. Let it shine!

As the light of Jesus shines through us, we can't help but impact our world. That light in the darkness not only gives God glory but also attracts people who don't yet know Jesus—so that our one light can become a whole, glowing kingdom for God.

Lord, help me live out the truth of that old children's song—to take my little light and let it shine all around me!

DECEMBER 28

GOD IS TRUSTWORTHY

This is our God! We trusted in him, and he saved us!

ISAIAH 25:9 NLT

Trust—once we've been betrayed—is not easily given. But know this: while the people in our lives may sometimes let us down, there is One who never does—our heavenly Father. When we choose to acknowledge Him as the Lord of our lives, when we trust Him to lead us in the way we should go, He is always faithful to follow through.

As you begin each new day, choose to "trust in the LORD with all your heart" (Proverbs 3:5), holding nothing back. Don't follow your own wisdom, follow His. Lean on the Lord's faithfulness, not your own wisdom. He will not let you fall (Psalm 37:24); indeed, He will bless you, so you can say with the Israelites, "We trusted in him, and he saved us!"

Father, when I struggle to trust You, help me remember all the times You've been faithful to keep Your promises to me.

DECEMBER 29

WALK WORTHY

Walk worthy of the Lord, fully pleasing Him, being fruitful in every good work and increasing in the knowledge of God.

COLOSSIANS 1:10

When we consider all the Lord has done for us, we want to please Him, to "walk worthy" of Him. But what exactly does that mean? And can we ever truly be worthy of God?

While we certainly cannot earn our way into God's grace, we can live in a way that brings joy to Him, rather than exasperation or grief. We please Him when we study His Word and explore His truths. We please God when we turn to Him as the source of our strength, endurance, patience, and joy. This is what it means to walk worthy of the Lord. It's not a dour, solemn sort of trudging, but rather a joyful journey toward our inheritance in heaven.

Father, place within my heart the desire to faithfully and joyfully serve You.

DECEMBER 30

FINISH HIS WORK

Being confident of this very thing, that He who has begun a good work in you will complete it until the day of Jesus Christ.

PHILIPPIANS 1:6

We tend to abandon our projects. We dive in, all excitement and good intentions. But when it gets to be messy or tiresome or too much trouble, we walk away.

Not God.

When we accept Jesus as our Savior and Lord, God begins a work in us, making us holy and molding us into who He created us to be. It's a process that occurs every day of our lives.

We'll never stop learning about God and our walk with Him. Our thoughts and actions take on a greater purpose as we allow the Lord to guide all we say and do, as we allow ourselves to be used to draw others to Him. In this you can be fully confident: God will finish this work He's begun in you.

God, forgive me for the times I am messy and tiresome and troublesome. I am so grateful You do not abandon Your work in me.

DECEMBER 31

A NEW WAY

"I will do a new thing, now it shall spring forth; shall you not know it? I will even make a road in the wilderness and rivers in the desert."

ISAIAH 43:19

It doesn't have to matter. That thing you did, those words you said, that situation you found yourself stuck in. Whether it was your own poor choice or someone else's, or simply a sinful world at work, this past year—or years—doesn't have to predict the coming year.

When you surrender your life to God, He begins making a new way for you. Remember, He's got a plan, and it's perfect (Jeremiah 29:11). And in His glorious wisdom, He even takes your past problems and mistakes and draws forth goodness from them (Romans 8:28).

There's no wilderness of sin too wild, no river of regrets too raging for the Lord. The new year is coming . . . and God will make a new way for you (Isaiah 43:16).

Lord, help me leave the past behind and embrace the new way You are making for me.